DAVENPORT'S MAINE WILLS AND ESTATE PLANNING LEGAL FORMS

ALEX RUSSELL
ROBERT MAXWELL

DAVENPORT'S MAINE WILLS AND ESTATE PLANNING LEGAL FORMS

2024 EDITION

written by attorneys
Alex Russell and Robert Maxwell

SEE BOOKS AND LEGAL FORMS AT
WWW.DAVENPORTPUBLISHING.COM

COPYRIGHT © 2024 -- ALEX RUSSELL

CREATIVE COMMONS LICENSE. This work is also licensed under a Creative Commons Attribution-NonCommercial-NoDerivatives 4.0 International License.

GOVERNMENT WORKS. No claim is made to copyright or ownership of government materials.

SOME STANDARD FORMS. No copyright or ownership is claimed of "standard" forms or leading forms for the state which are provided in this book, but fair use and privilege to use is claimed. Makers of such forms (often a state agency or hospital) have agreed by word, act, and implication the forms may be used and copied if no profit is sought and no substantial changes made to them. Such makers if not a lawyer or law firm are barred from profit or advantage in practicing law by making forms then limiting use. Forms and other related materials are used here for educational purposes only. Authors strongly believe in a religious duty to help people and do charity.

PUBLICATION DATA
(informal, library may use different data)

Names: Russell, Alex, 1972- author; Maxwell, Robert, 1960- author

Title: Davenport's Maine Wills And Estate Planning Legal Forms 2024 Edition

Other Titles: Davenport's Wills

Description: Davenport Publishing 2024

Suggested Identifiers: 9798360489696, LCCN 2021909030, 9798748423373

Subjects: LCSH: Wills--United States;
Wills--United States--Forms;
Estate Planning--United States;
Legal Forms

Classification: LFF KF755 .C55 2024 (or as library chooses)
DDC 346.73 Rus--dc24 (or as library chooses)

9 8 7 6 5 4 3 2 1 0 0 0 0 0 2 4

PERMISSION TO COPY AND USE BOOKS FOR FREE

To help people and groups the publisher and authors of the book allow mostly free use by giving all a "Creative Commons Attribution-NonCommercial-NoDerivatives 4.0 International License". Most users face no limit on copying, using, holding in library to loan out, or giving out copies.

Basically, as the image below shows, any copying or use is OK if it still shows it is by the authors, is non-commercial (nc) with no price charged, and has no derivatives (nd) so no big changes.

(This work licensed under a Creative Commons Attribution-NonCommercial-NoDerivatives 4.0 International License.)

TO GET COPIES OF BOOKS USE WWW.DAVENPORTPUBLISHING.COM OR AMAZON.COM.

EMAIL ANY QUESTIONS TO DAVENPORTPRESS@GMAIL.COM.

WARNING

THIS PUBLICATION IS NOT A SUBSTITUTE FOR LEGAL ADVICE. Publisher and authors say and warn this publication is not giving any legal, accounting, or other professional services or advice, which if wanted can be obtained by consulting in person an attorney or some other professional. **No attorney-client relationship or any relationship creating a duty or obligation is agreed to or created by the purchase or use of this publication or forms.**

**BOOKS AND FORMS FOR OTHER STATES ARE AVAILABLE,
SEE WWW.DAVENPORTPUBLISHING.COM FOR INFORMATION**

CHAPTER	TABLE OF CONTENTS	PAGE
CHAPTER 1 – LIST OF FORMS, BOOK BASICS, AND INFORMATION FORM		1
CHAPTER 2 – LEGAL TERMS AND BASIC PROPERTY LAW		5
CHAPTER 3 – WILL BASICS		7
CHAPTER 4 – WILL GIFTS INCLUDING RESIDUE CLAUSE		9
CHAPTER 5 – DEBT, MARRIAGE, AND YOUNG CHILD ISSUES		14
CHAPTER 6 – BASIC IDEAS ABOUT HEALTH CARE FORMS		17

AFTER DEATH FORMS

CHAPTER 7 – FORM 1: WILL (STANDARD)		18
CHAPTER 8 – FORM 2: WILL (GUARDIAN)		22
CHAPTER 9 – FORM 3: MAINE STATUTORY WILL		26
CHAPTER 10 – FORM 4: HANDWRITTEN WILL		33
CHAPTER 11 – FORM 5: SELF-PROVING AFFIDAVIT		35
CHAPTER 12 – FORM 6: TANGIBLE PERSONAL PROPERTY LIST		37

HEALTH CARE FORMS

CHAPTER 13 – FORM 7: POWER OF ATTORNEY FOR HEALTH CARE		39
CHAPTER 14 – FORM 8: DO NOT RESUSCITATE		44

GIVING POWER FORMS

CHAPTER 15 – FORM 9: DURABLE POWER OF ATTORNEY		49
CHAPTER 16 – FORM 10: POWER OF ATTORNEY OVER MINOR CHILDREN		52
CHAPTER 17 – FORM 11: GRANT OF CUSTODY AND CONTROL OF REMAINS AFTER DEATH		54

APPENDIX: HOW TO GET FORMS AND SAMPLE FILLED OUT FORMS		56

CHAPTER 1
LIST OF FORMS, BOOK BASICS, AND INFORMATION FORM

ESTATE PLANNING IS MOSTLY DOING SIMPLE THINGS IN 3 AREAS

This book lets a person in Maine do Estate Planning documents to do simple things like say what to do about a person's property, money, children, health care, funeral, and more if later they're absent, sick, or dead. The book has 11 legal forms for Maine but most people use just a few of the forms.

WILL RELATED FORMS

Form 1. Will (Standard) – also called a "Last Will and Testament" this lets a person control things after their later death especially gifts of property and money, and this Form 1 is the most used Will in this book.

Form 2. Will (Guardian) – this is a Will with part added to name a trusted person to if needed care for a minor child under 18 (like if both parents die), and also if needed care for a child's property and money.

Form 3. Maine Statutory Will – the state legislature put this Will form in state law for people to use, and it is inflexible but fairly reliable and simple, and people with less wealth or to save time sometimes use this.

Form 4. Handwritten Will – this Will skips the usual 2 witnesses which saves work, but all its words must be handwritten by the person doing the Will, and people with less wealth or to save time sometimes use this.

Form 5. Tangible Personal Property List – lets a person easily add gifts to occur after death, but it can only be used if a Will exists and can only cover "tangible personal property" like household items or vehicles.

Form 6. Self-Proving Affidavit – optional form done with a Will to later help show it was signed right.

HEALTH CARE FORMS

Form 7. Power Of Attorney For Health Care – lets a person name someone to later control health care if needed like if the person is later incapacitated and write health care instructions, and it also can cover ending care if later doctors think more care won't help an incapacitated person (called "Living Will" issues).

Form 8. Do Not Resuscitate – these are 2 forms that do serious act of immediately refusing most further care, and these are short so paramedics can read them fast and they can be used outside a care facility.

GIVING POWER FORMS

Form 9. Durable Power Of Attorney – lets power over money, property, and more be shared during life with a trusted person so they can do things to help.

Form 10. Power Of Attorney Over Minor Child – lets a parent share power over a minor child under 18 with someone so they can make decisions if needed like with health care, school, and discipline.

Form 11. Grant Of Custody And Control Of Remains After Death – lets a person be named to control funeral and related matters, usually done only if a person doesn't want closest family to do this.

BY LAW A PERSON CAN CONTROL THESE ISSUES BUT IT'S OFTEN NOT VITAL

Estate Planning is usually easy to do since by law a person mostly has full power to control these things. Given this usually judges, doctors, and other people mostly just ask: "Based on what a person wrote what did they likely want done?" It is also easy since simple documents can mostly be used and a few simple words can be written to do things. But in reality Estate Planning is often not worth spending much resources doing since it often doesn't greatly change the costs, taxes, delays, and later work in these areas. This is very true for young people under 40 unlikely to die or be ill soon. Many people focus more on getting life insurance.

BOOK USES EMPHASIS, UNDERLINING, AND SHOULD SUIT MOST PEOPLE

For emphasis paragraph titles, underlining, and boxes are used. This book capitalizes some legal words like Will, Testator, and Agent but this is optional. To save room some small words are skipped and end quote marks put before punctuation. This book covers the big Estate Planning ideas and main ways Maine law is different. This very short book can't cover all issues but should suit people without strange situations or wishes. Strange situations or wishes that may need research or a lawyer include: a) strange gift plans for property and money, b) wealth over $3 million, c) big medical concerns like extreme age, d) property or money going to a person with a disability or special needs, and e) wish to move or hide assets to qualify for government help.

MOST FORMS ARE STANDARD AND NOTARY AND WITNESSES MAY BE NEEDED

Legal forms are good at most things involved in Estate Planning and can make binding legal documents. Instead of forms a lawyer can be used but this can be costly, take months, and they can make mistakes. In life people often pick a cheap option. Often a hospital, charity, legislature, or agency has made a "standard form", and doctors, banks, and others may not like to use or see different forms. This book is mostly standard forms. Some documents need to be "witnessed", which is someone watching a form be signed who then signs too. Some documents need to be "notarized" where a person who is a "notary" sees it signed and notarizes it. A notary (also called "notary public") can be found using a phonebook, and are at some banks, brokers, law offices, courts, libraries, and mail-copy centers. A document signed in a foreign language is usually binding. When filling in form parts other than signatures this can be filled in by someone not signing including in pencil. People often try to keep the original and hand out copies. A person can have everyone sign many copies to have many ink signatures. A person "doing a legal document" and "doing a form" means the form is for them.

SOME LESS COMMON OR LESS USEFUL FORMS ARE NOT IN THIS BOOK

■ Some people do a "Pet Trust" to help a pet, but it's easier to just give money in a Will to who gets the pet.

■ Some people do a "Revocable Living Trust" so a Trust with a Trustee holds property or money during their life or later, mostly done to avoid small delays, costs, and work after death (by "avoiding probate"). But this is rare as it can require much work to move a person's property and money to a Trust and cause years of hassle.

■ "Childrens Trust" papers can be done so upon a death a Trust gets things for a minor child to manage till 18, but this is uncommon due to possible costs and hassles and since it rarely matters (as this book explains).

INFORMATION FORM CAN HELP TELL FAMILY AND FRIENDS THINGS

People can do some kind of "Information Form" so family or friends after a death will know helpful things. People can staple financial records and other pages to it. See form on the next pages to use if wanted.

ESTATE PLANNING HELPFUL INFORMATION

For more space attach copies of form or blank pages. Keep pages by Will or other place for Executor or family.

1. Personal Information (Name, Birthdate, Social Security number, special family details, other):

2. Real estate, vehicles, and other major tangible property (especially if people may not find them):

3. Non-tangible assets like stocks, accounts, investments, loans owed you, and business interests:

4. Possible income or insurance like pensions, retirement, disability, insurance, or contracts:

5. Debts owed by you like credit card, loan, student loan, mortgage, car loans, and accounts payable:

6. Names and information of professionals used (attorneys, accountants, brokers, doctors, others):

7. Computer passwords and helpful files, document places, and safes or safe-deposit boxes code/key:

8. Other helpful things, wishes for funeral, special requests, and last messages to family and friends:

CHAPTER 2
LEGAL TERMS AND BASIC PROPERTY LAW

THERE ARE BASIC TERMS AND IDEAS IN ESTATE PLANNING

Some legal terms and ideas are basic to Estate Planning.

■ "Estate Planning" is about people doing legal documents to control things if later absent, sick, or dead. After a document is done people are still mostly free to transfer property, instruct doctors, or change forms.

■ "Probate" is a legal process to do things after someone's death like transfer property, handle creditors, and authorize a Guardian. Due to changes in the law probate is now often informal, faster, and less costly.

■ A "Will" or "will" (this book uses upper case "W") is a legal document done to control issues after death. The phrase "Last Will And Testament" is used since a Testament use to be a separate page done with a Will. A "Codicil" document can be used to modify a Will but it is easier and legally safer to just re-do the whole Will.

■ An "Executor" is a person named in a Will to do things after someone's death. If no Will names someone a judge names an "Administrator" to do this. "Personal Representative" is a blanket term for both these 2.

■ A person doing a Will is called the "Testator" or "Will maker". Before about 1995 a woman Testator was often called a "Testatrix" and woman Executor called an "Executrix" but this is no longer often said or written.

■ If no valid Will is done a person is "intestate" and then a dead person's property and money is transferred to a spouse, children, and family as intestate law says. Some people a fine with this. This is covered later.

■ A person who died is called the "decedent" or "deceased". A person getting a Will gift is usually called a "recipient", "beneficiary", or "heir" if related (they "inherit"). "Survive" or "surviving" is to be alive after someone else died. The term "descendants" or "issue" usually means a person's children and grandchildren.

■ The words "subscribe" and "execute" means signing a document, and "acknowledgment" means admitting one signed. The term "respectively" in a document means "in the order just stated".

■ A person under age 18 is usually called a "minor" and often a parent or guardian helps them do things. A minor or other person not reasonably able to make wise decisions lacks "capacity" and is "incapacitated".

■ A document giving power to someone is often called a "Power of Attorney" where the "Principal" gives power to someone called the "Agent" or "Attorney-in-Fact" (but they need not be an actual attorney).

■ State law is the "Maine Statutes", sometimes called "revised" which means updated. Each law is usually called a "statute" shown by the "§" symbol. Each law can be cited by a few words and numbers, for example: "21 Maine Revised Statutes § 402". A form written into law for people to use if wanted is a "statutory form".

■ The "estate" or "probate estate" means all property and money of a dead person that at death or soon after didn't automatically legally go to new owners. Importantly, the estate is also the name for a temporary entity run by an Executor to do things after a death (it's like a small corporation that lasts a year or so).

PERSON CAN ONLY GIFT IN WILL WHAT THEY OWN AT DEATH

A person can only gift by Will things they own, so people should think about or research what they own. Basically by law a person usually owns all they earn as wages and salary, owns their share of income and profit tied to property they own, and owns or partly owns any things their money buys or improves. For items with "title" documents (real estate or vehicles) or where there is a "listed owner" (like accounts) the named persons are owners unless there are special circumstances. But a person during life is still free to do things, so people should try to notice if they sell or give away property they also name in a Will gift. Legally property is either: 1) "real property" which is land and buildings ("real estate"), 2) "fixtures" which are things tied to real property (like fences, cables, carpets, and wired-in appliances), or 3) "personal property" which is all else (like household items, clothes, tools, cars, jewelry, art, moneys, accounts, and stocks),

THINGS OWNED IN SPECIAL WAYS MAY LIMIT GIFTING IN A WILL

A person should consider if they own real estate or other property in special ownership ways which may limit gifting by Will. Laws vary in different states but some common special ways of ownership are:

- "joint tenant with right of survivorship" or similar legal options might be used in papers, so at a death property goes automatically to other named owners despite what a Will says (this is often how spouses hold a home);
- papers say a "life estate" exists, so then if a life of someone ends the other people in papers get item; and
- "Trust property" occurs if paperwork made a Trust entity and then property was transferred into it or this is set to occur, so then the Trust papers control where things put in the Trust go after someone's death.

Simple "joint ownership" with many owners can occur if people do joint papers, all agree to it, buy with joint funds, or if a gift was to many people. Wills <u>can</u> gift joint property, like "I give my half of boat to Ed Hu".

NON-PROBATE TRANSFERS THAT HAPPEN AUTOMATICALLY IGNORE A WILL

Importantly, some money or property of a decedent may automatically transfer on death or soon after to new owners if certain arrangements were made earlier. This is called "non-probate property". Such things transfer as arranged even if a Will names the same items. Examples are: a) a "designated beneficiary" form was done to name people to get an investment or account, b) transfer-on-death accounts were used, and c) real property is held by 2 people as "joint tenants with survivorship" or similar so at a death the surviving person gets things. Life insurance usually goes to the named beneficiary. Also, usually property in a Trust will ignore a Will and transfer as papers say. Trying to do non-probate transfers for all things is called "avoiding probate", but this is rarely done since it can be a hassle, has small benefits, and may fail People should consider non-probate transfers that will occur automatically at a death and consider what will be left.

USUALLY NO FEDERAL, MAINE, OR OTHER TAX IS OWED DUE TO A DEATH

Despite what many people think usually no tax is owed due to a death, including no inheritance, estate, or similar taxes. The "Federal Estate And Gift Tax" is only owed if a tax credit is used up that covers $13.99 million per person in 2025 and later. The Maine estate tax is only owed if a tax credit is used up that covers $6.8 million a person after 2023. A few states have taxes that may apply for things there if the owner dies, but they usually do not tax anything under $3 million.

CHAPTER 3
WILL BASICS

WILL LETS A PERSON CONTROL THINGS AFTER THEIR DEATH

A Will is a legal document done to control some things after a person's death. The phrase "Last Will And Testament" is used since a "Testament" was a separate page done with a Will to do some things. A person doing a Will is called the "Testator" or "Will maker". In Maine a Testator when signing must be at least age 18, of sound mind (rational with sufficient memory), and not be under duress (unfair pressure or threat).

THIS BOOK HAS 4 WILL FORMS TO PICK FROM AND USUALLY DO 1 WILL

This book has 4 Will forms to pick from and usually do 1. In this book Form 1 and Form 2 are more normal Wills (most people use these), Form 3 is the Statutory Will form found in state law to use if wanted, and Form 4 is a Handwritten Will a person must handwrite.

KEEP SIGNED WILL IN SAFE PLACE IT CAN BE FOUND AFTER A DEATH

A Will once done should be kept so it can be found after a death, like in a desk, drawer, safe, with a person, or less often a safe deposit box. It may help to tell family how to get a Will. Maine probate courts let a Will be filed during a person's life for safekeeping, but if people do a new Will they should remove the Will they filed.

A WILL USUALLY MUST BE SIGNED WITH 2 WITNESSES

WILL MUST SHOW IT'S A WILL AND USUALLY BE SIGNED WITH 2 WITNESSES

Usually a document to be a Will must show it is a Will by its words, and the person doing it must usually sign in front of 2 persons acting as witnesses who sign too. Some people modify a Will to have 3 or 4 witnesses just in case this helps later. A Will just spoken on a video or audio recording usually has no legal effect at all. As this book later covers Maine law does let witnesses be skipped if a Will is all handwritten.

WITNESSES SHOULD AT LEAST AGE 18 AND OFTEN NOT GETTING WILL GIFTS

A person to witness a Will must be at least age 18. It is best but not legally required a witness not be very old, live far away, or be named in a Will to be Executor, Guardian, or similar. Maine law unlike some states says a Will is still valid if a witness or their spouse are getting Will gifts. But many people just to avoid the appearance of misconduct pick witnesses who are "disinterested" which means they or a spouse are not named to get anything in a Will. Often witnesses are friends, neighbors, strangers, or family members.

TESTATOR AND 2 WITNESSES SIGN THE WILL WHEN TOGETHER IN 1 ROOM

A person usually signs a Will with 2 persons as witnesses who also sign while all are in 1 room and see others sign. People showing others an ID is not required but common. A Testator needn't initial Will pages. A Testator or witness usually use their full legal name unless they dislike and rarely use it. Witnesses only read the paragraph they sign. Some Wills have a witness print their name and address. Though not needed by Maine law often a Testator often says a thing like, "My name is ___ and this is my Will that I do voluntarily and ask you 2 people to witness". Some Testators chat with witnesses to help show they are of sound mind.

MOST WILLS SAY PEOPLE MAY LATER DO INFORMAL PROBATE

Most Wills very helpfully say later the family and friends may do "informal probate" which can avoid costs and delays. Informal probate often is done with just 1 court hearing and completed in well under 1 year.

MOST WILLS SAY TO SKIP COSTLY BOND FOR EXECUTOR AND OTHERS

Most Wills very helpfully say no "bond" or "surety" is needed for an Executor, Guardian, or similar. This is insurance against misconduct. A Testator doesn't want this since it's costly and they trust those they named.

OFTEN AT START OF A WILL A PERSON NAMES ANY SPOUSE AND CHILDREN

Many Wills start with a place for a Testator to name any current living spouse and children of any age. Natural or adopted children should be put here including any born outside marriage. People without this family can skip this or put "none". Not doing this may invalidate a Will by indicating a person lacks sufficient mental ability, or let a spouse or child not listed ask a judge to give them a share or all of the estate by claiming a Testator just forgot them. After listing family in a Will a Testator is often free to give them nothing.

CANCELING OLD WILLS IS USUALLY NOT A PROBLEM

So a new Will is followed old Wills should be canceled ("revoked") but this is easy. A new Will says old Wills are revoked to cancel them. Or people can revoke an old Will by writing "void" or "cancelled" or "X" on it. But usually crossing out just part of a Will has no effect and revoking a Will doesn't bring back an earlier Will.

A WILL NAMES AN EXECUTOR TO DO THINGS AFTER DEATH

A WILL NAMES SOMEONE TO BE EXECUTOR TO DO THINGS AFTER A DEATH

Usually a Will names someone as "Executor" to act after a death. The law gives Executors many helpful legal powers, like to handle debts, find and collect and give new owners property and money, and do probate If a Will fails to name an Executor a judge can pick someone, but family may argue about who to suggest. Note, the term "Personal Representative" and not Executor is now often used in Maine for the person doing things after a death, but these terms mostly mean the same thing. Will gifts can go to an Executor.

EXECUTOR CAN BE PAID AND ESTATE PAYS FOR EXECUTOR'S EXPENSES

Maine law says an Executor can ask to be paid. For example, an Executor may ask for $40/hour for 100 hours of work they did in a year, so ask to be paid $4000. In reality most Executors later skip asking for pay so as to not owe income tax and leave more resources in the estate to carry out Will gifts. Note, expenses an Executor has like for insurance, utilities, repairs, funeral, mortgage, attorneys, and probate costs are paid for with money or property of the estate. Any lawyer doing work is usually paid what an Executor agreed to.

EXECUTOR IS PERSON AT LEAST 18 AND SECOND PERSON RARELY NEEDED

A person to be Executor must be at least age 18 and usually not have a bad criminal record like a felony. The person not reside in Maine. Naming 2 people to both be Executor is allowed but rare due to the risk of arguments and delays, and since any 1 person named should be trusted. People can name a 2nd person to be Executor if the 1st person is not later available but most skip this since this is rare and a judge can just pick someone. To add a 2nd person a person could write: "or if they can't serve I name _____ to serve".

CHAPTER 4
WILL GIFTS INCLUDING RESIDUE CLAUSE

PRIMARY USE OF A WILL IS TO WRITE GIFTS TO HAPPEN AFTER DEATH

Most people use a Will mainly to legally say what happens to their property and money after their death, usually by writing down various Will gifts to occur when they die. Verbal and even writings about this are not usually valid if not in a written Will. A Will can control property acquired after it was signed. The end of this Chapter covers "intestate law" which says where a person's things go at death if no valid Will handles this.

GIFTING IN A WILL USING SIMPLE WORDS OFTEN IS BEST

Making gifts in a Will using simple words is often best, using words like "I give to" and "I gift to". This is legally fine and avoids confusing legal words like "bequest", "devise", and "legacy" which few people know.

A PERSON IS MOSTLY FREE TO GIFT THEIR THINGS AS WANTED

A person is mostly free to give at death their money and property as they want. But creditors a decedent owed money, a spouse, and minor children under age 18 may have some rights which this book later covers.

IN WILL CAN DO SPECIFIC GIFTS TO GIFT PARTICULAR PROPERTY

Most Wills have "specific gifts" to gift particular things. Specific gifts can be any property, like "I give boat to Ed Blom" and "I give UBank account #84553873 to Sue Wu". If a gift is not clear the law assumes all of a kind of thing is given, like "I give jewelry to Ann Po" means all jewelry. But gifting specific property can have surprises like value of items can change, or a Will gift may later fail to occur if property is not owned at death.

IN WILL CAN DO GENERAL GIFTS LIKE OF MONEY

Wills can do "general gifts" where what is gifted is not particular property but can be flexibly chosen, like "I give 1 of my 3 cars to Ed Po" which lets an Executor pick which car. The usual general gift is money, like "I give $5 to Ed Hu". Money gifts are easy to write, let equal gifts be made, and are legally safer for many reasons. To carry out money gifts an Executor usually uses accounts or sells some property in the estate.

PROPERTY OR MONEY IN A JOINT GIFT GOES TO MULTIPLE PEOPLE TO GET

The same thing in a "joint gift" can go to many people to each get a part. For example, "I give all hats to Ann Lu and Sue Fox" means each person owns part of each item. People later can agree how to split things or let Executor says. If a person in a joint gift has died their part often transfers as the Residue Clause says. If people don't want recipients of the same gift to get it equally then percentages can be used tto make unequal gifts, including in the Residue Clause, like "I give boat 90% to Ed Doe and 10% to Ann Fox".

GIFTS IN WILL CAN GO TO A GROUP OR CLASS OF PEOPLE

To save work a Will gift can go to a group or class of people like certain family <u>if who is meant is later easy to determine</u>. People can say roughly how <u>much in total</u> is gifted to be clearer. Examples are: "I give $10 to each person on my 2018 soccer team" and "I give $10 to each of my grandkids so this is about $100 in total."

RESIDUE CLAUSE GIFTING ALL LEFT IS MAIN WAY USED TO GIFT THINGS

THE RESIDUE CLAUSE IS CATCH-ALL THAT HELPS GIFT ANYTHING LEFT

Most Wills by their end have a Residue Clause to gift any property or money not gifted earlier in a Will or used in other ways. Things transferred this way is called the "Residue". Many people gift most their money and property this way by intentionally not mentioning in a Will most things so the Residue Clause handles it. This avoids need to describe things and has less legal risk. After applying a Residue Clause if anything is somehow left then by law a decedent's closest heirs-at-law get things (this is their closest family).

USUAL RESIDUE CLAUSE HAS 2 PARTS

A short 2 part Residue Clause is usual and is used in this book's Will forms, and it has:

1) 1st space to name 1 or more persons to get things if they survive Testator (many name a spouse or closest family here), and if several people are named but only some survive then survivors split things, and

2) 2nd space to name persons to get things if all in the 1st space don't survive (many people name next close family or friends in this space), and if a person in 2nd space has died their descendants get their share.

Note, in the 2 part clause writing the same thing in both spaces or skipping the 1st part to just use the 2nd spot is legally fine and is done by a few people who think this better says what they want done.

EXAMPLE OF 2 PART RESIDUE CLAUSE:

"RESIDUE CLAUSE: I give money and property not gifted earlier, the residue:
   a) to   __John Paul Doe my husband__   who survive me with persons just named who survive me taking the share of non-survivors, then if anything remains
   b) to   __Sam Doe, Beth Wu, and Greta Fisher__   and if any of those just named do not survive me their part goes to their lineal descendants per stirpes."

In this example if John Paul Doe has survived he gets all things, but if John Paul Doe hasn't survived and also Sam Doe hasn't survived and he left 2 daughters then those 2 daughters split the 1/3 share of his (so get 1/6 each) and the other 2 persons in the second part Beth Wu and Greta Fisher get 1/3 each.

PEOPLE CAN PUT SAME THING IN PARTS, OR SKIP PART, OR USE PERCENTAGE

Some people put the same 1 person in both parts of a Residue Clause, to fully ensure that 1 person or if they later die their descendants will get things. Or a person with no spouse may skip the Residue Clause 1st part and in the 2nd part put their children (including any who died who had a child), so all branches of a family get an equal share. *See Appendix.* Many people use percentages in the Residue Clause. *See Appendix.*

SOME PEOPLE CHANGE A RESIDUE CLAUSE TO HAVE 1 PART

Some people change a Residue Clause to have just 1 part since this can gift more equally and be easier to understand. *See example in Appendix.* For example a Residue Clause can be made to say:

"The rest, residue, and remainder of my estate, and anything else, I give to _____ who survive me and if any of those just named do not survive me their part goes to their lineal descendants per stirpes."

MUST SUFFICIENTLY DESCRIBE NAMES AND PROPERTY IN A WILL

PUTTING NAMES OF PEOPLE OR GROUPS IN A WILL IS FAIRLY EASY

Putting names in Wills is fairly easy. A judge or Executor assume a person in a Will meant people they are closest to, so common names are OK unless 2 friends or family have the same name. Details can help if names won't be recognized or to be friendly, like "I give $5 to waitress Ann Fox" or "I give $5 to pal Ed Wu". If people used nicknames "also known as" or "a/k/a" may help, like "I give $5 to John Smith a/k/a Big Fish". Gifts can go to a charity, government, or group, like "I give $10 to The Salvation Army, "I give $8 to York County Library, Maine", and "I give $5 to Wix Church, Rex, TX". People can phone for a charity's name.

PUTTING DESCRIPTIONS OF ITEMS IN WILL GIFTS IS FAIRLY EASY

Describing items in gifts is easy since people rarely own similar items. Often fine are gifts like: "I give ax to Ed Wu" and "I give big table to Ann Fox". It's OK to gift by category or list, like: "I give tools to Sam Lee" and "I give cow, van, and harp to Sue Hill". Financial assets can use plain words, like "bank accounts" or "stocks", but details can help, like: "US Bank account ending #1511". Gifting using a location is riskier as judges will ignore Will gifts if it seems items were placed to affect gifting and no "independently significant" life reason. So, "I give Ed Po items in safe and desk" judges might not follow, but "I give Ed Po hats in attic" likely is OK.

DESCRIBING REAL PROPERTY IS HARD IF NOT USING RESIDUE OR TITLE

The easier, legally safer way to transfer real property (real estate) at death is: 1) do nothing specific so it's handled by a Will Residue Clause, or 2) have a lawyer or agent put names in a deed or similar document so then named persons legally get things at someone's death. Most use these 2 ways to transfer real property.

Gifting real property other ways is harder though possible. Helpfully a Will gift of real property described by location legally does gift all land, buildings, and fixtures located there with no need to describe what's there.

It is possible to gift real property at a particular address with very plain words, like a house, fixtures, and land can be fully given by something like: "I give 81 Maxwell Street, Augusta, Maine, to Mary Ann Brown".

People can do a blanket gift giving all of a kind of property, like, "I give all real property and fixtures in York County, Maine to Ann Ivy Hill " or "I give all furniture and all bank accounts to Eric Paul Carlson".

Giving real property in a Will using a "legal description" is how many lawyers do it, but this can be hard to do. If using a legal description people must copy without mistakes the full legal description of maybe many lines into a Will with no abbreviation at all. A legal description might be found on a deed or on mortgage papers. Legal descriptions may refer to a "lot" or "blocks" on a map which is recorded in land records of a county, or it may refer to a path around the land borders with various angles, distances, and iron stakes.

CAN LEAVE SOME WILL GIFT AREAS BLANK OR WRITE TO SAY SKIP GIFTS

A person can choose to not use some gifts areas in a Will legal form, like by just leaving areas blank, writing things like "SKIPPED" or "NONE", or using a computer to delete some gift lines. Judges and others usually do not care about neatness or empty spaces in Wills, and will follow whatever parts are filled in.

AFTER A DEATH FAMILIES OFTEN LET PEOPLE TAKE ITEMS UNOFFICIALLY

Many families unofficially let people take items in ways a dead person said, showed by stickers, or wrote on a note. If anyone objects a judge often has the Will and law be followed fully but later people can retransfer items.

CONDITIONS ON WILL GIFTS ARE RARE DUE TO POSSIBLE PROBLEMS

Putting conditions on a gift, like "I give Ann Poe $90 if she graduates college", can cause problems like years of delay, risk of lawsuits, and big attorney's fees. Due to all this conditions are rarely put on Will gifts.

MOST WILLS HAVE A MISCELLANEOUS PART WITH HELPFUL LANGUAGE

Most Wills have a "Miscellaneous" page with legal language that might help avoid later legal problems.

LATER DIVORCE OR MURDER CANCELS WILL GIFTS TO THE ACTING PERSON

If a person divorces or murders a Testator then by state law usually all Will gifts to them are cancelled.

OPTIONS EXIST TO HANDLE RARE CASE PERSON IN A WILL GIFT DIES

PERSON IN WILL GIFT USUALLY MUST SURVIVE OR GIFT DOES NOT OCCUR

Though rarely an issue, many Wills like this book's Will forms say a person named in a Will gift must survive (live past) the Testator or the gift will not later occur unless gift language specifically says different. If survival isn't required like this then what occurs can be unclear (for many reasons like certain state laws). Most people if they see a person in a gift has died just re-do a Will or trust a Residue Clause to handle it.

SOME PEOPLE ADD "ALTERNATE BENEFICIARY" MAYBE FOR SPECIAL ITEMS

Some people to handle if a person named in a Will gift dies maybe put for special items an alternate beneficiary, like for example: "I give oak table to Ed Wu but if they don't survive me to Ben Fox".

IF PERSON IN WILL GIFT DIES IT CAN GO TO "LINEAL DESCENDANTS"

A Will gift can say it goes to a person but if they don't survive the Testator then say the gift goes to the person's "lineal descendants". Descendants are a person's children and grandchildren. Also, the term "per stirpes" is often used to say to give to each family branch equally. An example shows how this works:

A Will may say: "All clothes to Sue Wu but if they don't survive to their lineal descendants per stirpes", and this means if Sue Wu has died and her son Ken Wu is living and her other son Ben Wu has died but left 2 children then, legally, by law Ken Wu himself gets 50% and Ben Wu's 2 children each get 25%.

HELPFUL LAWS OFTEN REQUIRE PERSON SURVIVE 120 HOURS TO GET GIFT

Laws in most states say a person dying within 120 hours of someone is seen as having died earlier, so often a Will gift to them is ignored. This book's Wills also at the end say this. This avoids legal problems like need to know exact time of death and, also, having an item go through many probate legal cases over years.

INTESTATE LAW CONTROLS THINGS NOT HANDLED BY A WILL OR SIMILAR

State "intestate" law starting at 18-C Maine Statutes § 2-102 says if a person dies without a valid Will or if anything is left after Will and transfers occur then certain surviving (living) family get money and property. Many people like how intestate law gives things and choose to skip a Will, but a Will can have other benefits. Note, the term "descendants" means a person's children and grandchildren, and if someone has died who would have got an intestate share often their descendants under intestate law get that share in their place. Maine intestate law if it applies basically says, in order:

SOME DESCENDANTS (CHILDREN OR GRANDCHILDREN)

1) if decedent (the person who died) left surviving (living) descendants but no spouse, then decedent's descendants gets the estate (all money and property of the decedent that after death did not transfer);

2) if decedent left a spouse and descendants and all descendants also are spouse's descendants (and the spouse has no other surviving descendants), then the spouse gets the estate;

3) if decedent left a spouse and descendants and all descendants also are spouse's descendants but the spouse has other descendants not shared with decedent, then the spouse gets the first $100,000 plus 1/2 of the balance of the estate, and remainder of the estate goes to decedent's descendants;

4) if decedent left a spouse and descendants and some of the descendants aren't spouse's descendants, then the spouse gets 1/2 of the estate, and then decedent's descendants get the remainder of the estate;

SPOUSE BUT NO DESCENDANTS

5) if decedent left a spouse but no descendants or parents, then the spouse gets the estate;

6) if decedent left a spouse and some parents but no descendants, then the spouse gets the first $300,000 plus 3/4 of the balance of the estate, and then the parents get the remainder of the estate;

NO SPOUSE AND NO DESCENDANTS

7) if decedent left surviving parents but no spouse or descendants, then parents get all of the estate;

8) if decedent left no surviving spouse or descendants or parents, then the next closest family to decedent get the estate starting with brothers and sisters and then going out to less close relations to a degree; and

9) if none of the above persons survive the decedent, then the estate goes to the state of Maine.

CHAPTER 5
MARRIAGE, DEBT, AND YOUNG CHILD ISSUES

THIS CHAPTER COVERS CERTAIN ISSUES THAT SOME PEOPLE CAN SKIP
This chapter covers marriage, debt, and young child issues, <u>and some people can skip parts of this</u>.

DEBT ISSUES

PAYING DECEDENT'S DEBTS MAY USE UP RESOURCES AND REDUCE GIFTS
If a decedent had debts then creditors owed may ask a judge to be paid from decedent's money or property <u>before</u> Will gifts and certain transfers occur. How debts are paid is set by state law and a Will need not describe this. Funds to pay debts comes from decedent's money and property so may affect (in order) the Will Residue, Will general gifts, Will specific gifts, and non-probate transfers. Probate, health care, taxes, and funeral costs have some priority to be paid first. But for many reasons often not all debts are paid. <u>People should consider how paying debts may use up money or property, leaving less to carry out Will gifts</u>. A spouse and family usually aren't liable for decedent's debts unless they actually guaranteed or co-signed.

SECURED DEBTS LIKE MORTGAGE OR VEHICLE LIEN ARE NOT PAID OFF
Laws in most states say <u>do not pay off secured debts on property of a decedent</u> like a house mortgage or vehicle lien even if other debts are paid by Executor or in probate. This avoids using up estate resources on paying these usually big debts and leaves more estate resources to carry out Will gifts and other transfers. Due to this, all this book's Will forms say do not usually pay off any secured debts. But if a Testator wants they can 1) put in a Will an order to pay (like, "Executor pay off the house mortgage"), or 2) gift enough money to pay off a secured debt to the person getting the property. Most banks let the new owners after a death keep paying monthly any secured debt like a mortgage or lien.

FAMILY RIGHTS MAY BE USED TO GET FAMILY THINGS BEFORE DEBTS
Most states have "Family Rights" a decedent's surviving spouse or children can claim, and this helpfully may let them get things even <u>before most debts of decedent are paid</u> and even <u>before Will gifts</u>.

<u>First</u>, so family have things to use to live the law in Maine gives a spouse, or if there's no spouse any children of decedent, the "<u>Exempt Property Right</u>" to get $15,000 of a decedent's household items and vehicles (or if there is not enough property then from decedent's money). See 18-C Maine Statutes § 2-402. Many states have this. To the extent possible family must pick items to get that are not mentioned in specific gifts in a decedent's Will. Family can even try to keep even more of decedent's property by claiming decedent gifted them various things.

<u>Second</u>, the law in Maine gives a spouse, or if there's no spouse then any dependent children, the right to get a "<u>Family Allowance</u>" to support family during any probate, and often a lump sum of $27,000 is paid to family from decedent's money and property. See 18-C Maine Statutes § 2-404. Many states have a similar right.

<u>Third</u>, Maine law lets a "Small Estate Affidavit" be used to get closest family the ownership of most things if the decedent's estate has under $49,700 (in 2024 and later) of money and property (but usually there can be no real property). See 18-C Maine Statutes § 3-1201. This often can be done without paying decedent's creditors.

Fourth, many states give a surviving spouse or young children a right to get (or stay in for years) the house or mobile home owned by a decedent under a "Homestead Law". Maine mostly does not have this but gives to a spouse or dependent children a "Homestead Allowance" of $22,500 to be paid from property and money in the decedent's estate. If possible family must pick items to get that are not mentioned in specific gifts in a Will. Of course often a person during life does papers so a spouse or children will get the house or mobile home, including by making them "joint tenants with right of survivorship" on a deed. Note, normally creditors without a mortgage have no power over a homestead property going to family. No matter what a spouse or children living in a home may be a hassle to remove. So family don't try to cause legal trouble about a house usually a person gives a house mostly to a spouse or young children. Some people may want to do other research.

MARRIAGE ISSUES

MAINE USES SEPARATE PROPERTY LAW FOR SPOUSES

Maine like most states uses the Separate Property Law system that says a married person mostly owns their money and property separately and not jointly with a spouse. Due to this a married person is usually free to sell during life or gift by Will most their money or property and usually don't have to involve a spouse. But joint ownership by 2 spouses and not separate ownership can arise in other ways, like by agreement, both spouses paying part of the purchase price, if a gift was to both spouses, or if paperwork calls it joint.

COMMUNITY PROPERTY LAW APPLIES IN OTHER STATES FOR SPOUSES

There are 9 states mostly in the Western U.S. that use the Community Property Law system for any spouses (Arizona, California, Louisiana, Idaho, Nevada, New Mexico, Texas, Washington, and Wisconsin). This says property or money is owned 50/50 by spouses as Community Property if it's from mental or physical work while married (like wages or salary) or if property is bought or improved using any existing Community Property. In rare cases people recently moving from these states may face legal issues.

JOINT WILL OR SIMILAR BOTH SPOUSES SIGN IS NOT RECOMMENDED

Some couples who worry a lot try to sign a "Joint Will" or a "Contract To Make A Will" done by a lawyer which says spouses give all to the other if they die first, then says last living spouse gives to all children equally, and usually says a spouse may not change this. This is banned in some states and is rarely used.

SPOUSE CAN SEEK ELECTIVE SHARE INSTEAD OF FOLLOWING THE WILL

Many states including Maine give a spouse if unhappy with what a Will gifts them a right to pick (elect) an "Elective Share" of their spouse's property and money instead. This is done for fairness to a spouse and so early divorce isn't seen as needed to be financially secure. Maine sets the Elective Share as a 1/2 share of decedent's money and property with small modifications. To help a surviving spouse in some cases the Elective Share by law can cover things a spouse gave away recently and certain things not fully owned. If an Elective Share is used then any Will gifts to the spouse are not done, but Will gifts to other people are carried out like normal unless the property and money is needed to satisfy the Elective Share to the spouse. Because of all this usually a married person gifts by Will and other ways mostly to their spouse (like at least 50%) to avoid a spouse being upset and using an Elective Share and other legal options.

YOUNG CHILD ISSUES

WILL CAN NAME A GUARDIAN TO CARE FOR YOUNG CHILD

If a parent dies with a child under age 18 then any other natural or adopted parent (but not a step-parent) almost always automatically gets control of the child's care (including health care, school, and home issues). This won't occur only if the other parent will be unavailable a long time or is proven unfit in court which is rare. But just in case it is later needed (like later both parents die) a Will often names a healthy and willing relative or friend as "Guardian" to give this care for a young child. Some states call this a "Guardian of the Person".

WILL CAN NAME A CONSERVATOR TO MANAGE CHILD'S PROPERTY

Since a child until age 18 can't legally easily control property including money a Will often names a person to be "Conservator" to have the job of managing a young child's property and money. Many states call this a "Guardian of the Estate" or "Guardian of Property". This person decides each year how to use property and money on a child's needs (like on school, living, and health care) and then usually at age 18 anything left goes to the child. A person paying things for a child can ask to be paid back. A judge often holds a yearly hearing on spending. As a nice 2nd option to avoid work and costs most Wills say an Executor may name a person including themselves as "Custodian" to manage things under the new Uniform Transfers To Minors Act.

MOST WILLS NAME 1 PERSON TO CARE FOR CHILD AND THEIR PROPERTY

This book's Will forms and most parents name the same 1 person to care for a child and also manage a child's property and money. People can change a Will to name different people for the 2 positions, but this is rarely worth it since parents dying is rare, rarely do children get much, a person smart enough to handle a child often can handle money, and naming different people can lead to arguments and even costly lawsuits between people. Will gifts can go to someone named to be a Guardian or Conservator.

PERSON TO HELP A CHILD MUST BE AT LEAST 18

A person to serve in a position helping a child in Maine must be at least age 18 but they needn't live here. Later usually a judge can't think the person is unfit to serve, which usually means no serious criminal felony or history of abuse or fraud. The choice by the last living parent is usually followed. If no Will names a person for a position or they're unavailable a judge can pick someone, but family may argue about who to suggest. Naming 2 people to act at the same time in the same position is rare since 2 persons may argue and any 1 person named should be smart enough to act alone. In rare cases a married couple is named for the same position but there can be problems if they divorce or disagree. Some Wills add a 2nd person to serve if the 1st person named is later not available, like: "or if they are later unable to serve I name _____ to serve"). But most people skip naming a fallback person since it is rarely needed, if a problem is seen a Will can be redone by a person, and a judge can just pick someone if needed.

NAMING PERSONS TO HELP CHILD RARELY MATTERS

A child under 18 having parents die is rare so parents shouldn't worry much about naming people to help. A good U.S. study looked at 72,240 people under age 18 and found only 2014 had lost 1 parent (so 2.78%) and only 97 had lost 2 parents (so a very small 0.13%). *Parent Mortality Census SIPP Paper #288.*

CHAPTER 6
BASIC IDEAS ABOUT HEALTH CARE FORMS

THERE ARE SOME BASIC IDEAS ABOUT HEALTH CARE FORMS

Some ideas help people understand health care forms.

■ By law people controls their own health care by telling medical personnel what they want unless they are "incapacitated" by insufficient ability to a) communicate verbally or by notes, b) be rational, or c) be conscious. Most people keep control of their own care till death or till no big treatment options remain, but some people worry they may be incapacitated a long time so want to do health care forms.

■ Legal documents that help control health care are usually called "Advanced Directives".

■ If an adult 18 or older becomes incapacitated the adult's closest family like spouse or adult child usually can make emergency decisions. But later they usually must then rush to a judge to get further power if no legal document gives them more power over health care.

■ In legal documents a person can be named to have control of health care if needed. This person is often called the "Health Care Agent", "Health Care Attorney-in-Fact", "Health Care Advocate", or a similar name.

■ In legal documents people can write medical instructions doctors, family, and other people must obey.

■ Parents even without legal documents mostly have full power over health care of children under age 18, and the only exception is teens have some freedom to pick their own family planning or gender related care.

■ Some married people do documents to give a spouse power over medical care if they are incapacitated. Some adults especially to age 25 do documents to give this power to parents. The young are less often sick.

■ Pain relief like pain drugs or comfort care is still given even if documents say to stop or limit other care.

■ Most people only do 1 legal document about health care that often names someone to control health care if needed and has a spot for basic instructions (this is sometimes called a "Health Care Power of Attorney").

■ For the rare times stopping health care seems more likely to matter (like due to extreme illness or old age):

-- most people do nothing special and trust family or Health Care Agent to wisely decide when to stop care (they can weigh many factors like pain, cost, likely difficulty of treatment, beliefs, and chances of recovery);

-- a few people do a serious document to say to stop most health care if later doctors think an incapacitated person has very bad health and more medical care likely won't help (sometimes this is called a "Living Will";

-- a few people do a serious document to say starting immediately to not give most medical care (often this is called a "Do-Not-Resuscitate" if about resuscitation, or called a "Physician's Order" if about many treatments).

CHAPTER 7
FORM 1: WILL (STANDARD)

FORM 1 IS A STANDARD WILL THAT IS FLEXIBLE BUT WITHOUT A GUARDIAN

Form 1 is a flexible Will that lets a person control things after their death. This form has no part about naming a Guardian for children so is for someone with no child under age 18. The phrase "Last Will And Testament" is used since long ago a "Testament" was a page done with a Will to do some legal things.

FORM IS A WILL WITH SEVERAL PARTS INCLUDING A GUARDIAN PART

The form starts with lines for a person to put their name (a full legal name is best but not required) and place of main residence (most put a county but some put a city). The Will is still valid if people later move.

Paragraph 1, "List Of Spouse And Children", is where a person write the names of any living spouse and children they have, or if none maybe write "none". This helps show a person has enough memory and mental ability to do a Will. Not listing a living spouse or child here can let an omitted person ask a judge to give them a share or all of a Testator's property and money by claiming they were accidently forgotten.

Paragraph 2, "Gifts", has many spaces to make either specific gifts of particular property or general gifts like of money. People can delete, copy and paste to add more, or leave blank these gift lines.

Paragraph 3, "Separate Writings", says to follow any separate writings done apart from the Will that gifts tangible personal property in manner allowed by state law.

Paragraph 4, "Residue", has a Residue Clause to say any property and money left after other Will parts and other transfers is to be distributed in the way a person wrote in the blank parts of this paragraph.

Paragraph 5, "Administration", names a person to be Personal Representative to do things after a person's death (in the past the similar term Executor was used in Maine for the person doing this).

Paragraph 6, "Miscellaneous", has paragraphs of legal language to help avoid certain legal issues.

Last is a paragraph for the person doing the Will to put the date and sign, and paragraph for 2 witnesses to put the date, sign, and print the addresses they live at. The person doing a Will is called the "Testator"

USUAL RESIDUE CLAUSE HAS 2 PLACES TO NAME PERSONS TO GET THINGS

In a Will "Residue Clause" anything left over after other Will parts is transferred as the clause directs. Many people use a Residue Clause to gift most their things. In this Will form's Residue Clause there is:

1) a 1st space to name 1 or more persons to get the Residue, and if any named here have died before the Will maker then other persons named here in this 1st space take the dead person's share, and

2) a 2nd space to name people to get things if all people named in the 1st space have died, and if any people named in the 2nd space have died their shares go to "lineal descendants" like their children.

People often put in the 1st space a spouse or closest family or friends, and in 2nd space next closest people.

TESTATOR AND 2 WITNESSES WHILE TOGETHER SIGN WILL

This Will after being filled out (except bits intentionally left blank) must be signed by the person doing the Will (the "Testator") in front of at least 2 persons acting as witnesses at least age 18 who then also sign.

LAST WILL AND TESTAMENT

I, _____, of _____, Maine, do revoke all prior Wills and testamentary documents and do make, publish, and declare this as my Will. I am of sound mind and under no duress or undue influence and acting voluntarily.

1. LIST OF SPOUSE AND CHILDREN. To help show I am mentally competent and have sufficient memory to make a Will I wish to list any living spouse and living children I now have. I currently have the following living spouse and living children:
_____
_____.

2. GIFTS. I give these gifts in this Will, but to get a gift in this section the recipient must survive me except as otherwise stated below.

I give _____ to _____.

I give _____ to _____.

I give _____ to _____.

I give _____ to _____.

I give _____ to _____.

I give _____ to _____.

I give _____ to _____.

I give _____ to _____.

3. SEPARATE WRITINGS. I may do writings separate from this Will to gift tangible personal property as allowed by state law, and all such writings should be followed. But any such writing not found within 90 days of my death is canceled and has no effect. A gift in such a writing to a person who does not survive me is canceled and has no effect. This Will does not revoke any such writings that now exist.

4. RESIDUE. I give the rest and residue and remainder of my estate, my money and property of any kind and nature, and anything I have an interest in so long as it was not transferred by other Will provisions (all of which is called the "residue"), as follows:
  a) to _____ who survive me with persons just named who survive me taking the share of non-survivors, then if anything remains
  b) to _____ and if any of those just named do not survive me their part goes to their lineal descendants per stirpes.

5. ADMINISTRATION. I name, nominate, and appoint _____
as Personal Representative including for me, my Will, and my estate.

6. MISCELLANEOUS. The following applies to this Will and generally.
   In this Will no part left unfilled is a mistake including spaces in the residue clause.
   The facts support and I want Maine state law to apply to this Will and my estate.
   I order that my just debts, funeral and related expenses, and taxes be paid as soon after my death as practical but only those items my Personal Representative chooses to pay.
   Priority of Will gifts of the same type is based on the order they are written.
   The words "give" and "gift" also means a devise, bequest, grant, legacy, or similar.
   I am intentionally not providing by Will or other ways for some family, including I am not providing for some children of mine and also children of a deceased child of mine.
   If a gift Will reasonably mentions survival then survival is an absolute condition and anti-lapse laws or similar provisions have no effect and without survival the gift lapses. Unless a Will gift specifies otherwise if a Will gift goes to multiple recipients if any do not survive me the part to them lapses and instead goes to other surviving recipients.
   No earlier money transfer reduces a Will gift unless I always called it a loan or similar.
   In this Will any gender or gendered word includes all genders, and the singular includes the plural and vice versa, and "they" can mean a single person or many persons.
   Unless a Will specifically says otherwise a secured debt including a mortgage or lien shall not be paid off including by a Personal Representative or in probate, and a recipient of a Will gift of property takes it subject to debts. Also, no recipient of property who may lose it or who pays to keep it may have my estate or others pay or do exoneration.
   If at death I no longer have an item in a specific gift the gift is void and extinguished.
   I request and authorize any informal, summary, and quick probate or similar action. Any Personal Representative may act independently with no supervision of any court, including independent administration, and with no inventory, appraisal, or other action.
   I give any Personal Representative the a) fullest authority, discretion, and powers allowed by state law, b) power to lease, sell, mortgage, convey, or keep property including real property in a manner and time they deem helpful or proper, and c) authority to settle or pay claims or debts in the time and manner they choose. Any Personal Representative or other fiduciary shall have all powers and authorities conferred by statute or common law in any jurisdiction they may act.
   Any Guardian of any type, Conservator, Custodian, or other person managing a minor's property or money may use or invade the principal and sell property without court action. A person named to manage things for a minor shall do this in similar roles outside Maine.
   If context permits the terms Personal Representative and Executor and Administrator are interchangeable, Conservator and Guardian of the Estate and Guardian of Property and Custodian are interchangeable, and residue and residuary are interchangeable. Any such person may stand in the place of and have all powers like the others named here.
   The residue includes lapsed or failed gifts, insurance paid to the estate, digital assets,

inheritances owed me, and all I had power of appointment or testamentary disposition over.

Any Personal Representative may access, manage, delete, modify, transfer, and otherwise control any digital accounts and assets I had any interest in or power over.

Any Personal Representative, Executor, Administrator, Guardian of any type like for a person or estate, Conservator, Custodian, and any other fiduciary under this Will or otherwise shall qualify and serve without bond, surety, security, surety bond, or similar.

If evidence does not show it likely a person survived me by 120 hours (5 days) then for this Will and my estate they shall be deemed in all ways as having died before me.

If part of this Will is by law invalid or unenforceable other provisions remain in effect.

Any Personal Representative may at any time transfer money or property of a minor under age 18 to a Custodian to serve under the Maine Uniform Transfers to Minors Act or similar law anywhere, and may pick a person to be Custodian including themselves.

TESTATOR

IN WITNESS WHEREOF, I declare and publish that this instrument is my Will which I make as Testator, that I do this as a free and voluntary act for the purposes expressed therein, that I am at least 18 years of age and of sound mind and under no constraint or undue influence, and I do sign this instrument voluntarily as my Will in the presence and sight of each of the persons acting as witnesses who are named and who sign below, this _____ day of _____, 20___.

_____
Testator signature

WITNESSES

We, the persons signing below, declare that in the presence and sight of each of us persons that _____ as Testator did voluntarily publish, declare, and sign the foregoing instrument as the Will of the Testator, that to the best of our knowledge the Testator is at least 18 years of age and of sound mind and under no constraint or undue influence, that each of us persons who sign below is at least 18 years old and fully competent to act as witnesses, and that in the presence and sight of Testator and each other we sign our names to witness this Will at the Testator's request.

_____ _____
Signature of Witness #1   Address of Witness #1

_____ _____
Signature of Witness #2   Address of Witness #2

CHAPTER 8
FORM 2: WILL (GUARDIAN)

FORM 2 IS A WILL WITH GUARDIAN PART FOR PEOPLE WITH YOUNG CHILD

Form 2 is a Will with a Guardian part for a person with any minor children under age 18. The phrase "Last Will And Testament" is used since a "Testament" was a separate page done with a Will to do things.

FORM IS A WILL WITH SEVERAL PARTS INCLUDING A GUARDIAN PART

The form starts with lines for a person to put their name (a full legal name is best but not required) and place of main residence (most put a county but some put a city). The Will is still valid if people later move.

Paragraph 1, "List Of Spouse And Children", lets a person write the names of any living spouse and children they have, or if none maybe write "none". This helps show a Testator has enough mental ability and memory to do a Will. Not listing a living spouse or child here can cause legal problems.

Paragraph 2, "Gifts", has many spaces to make either specific gifts of particular property or general gifts like of money. People can delete, copy and paste to add more, or leave blank these gift lines.

Paragraph 3, "Separate Writings", says to follow any separate writings done apart from the Will that gifts tangible personal property in manner allowed by state law.

Paragraph 4, "Residue", has a Residue Clause to say any property and money left after other Will parts and other transfers is to be distributed in the way a person wrote in the blank parts of this paragraph.

Paragraph 5, "Administration", names a person to be Personal Representative to do things after a person's death (in the past the similar term Executor was used in Maine for the person doing this).

<u>**Paragraph 6, "Guardian"**, names a person as Guardian of the Person to care for minor children under 18 if needed (like if both parents die) and as Conservator to manage property and money of children.</u>

Paragraph 7, "Miscellaneous", has paragraphs of legal language to help avoid certain legal issues.

Last is a paragraph for the person doing the Will to put the date and sign, and paragraph for 2 witnesses to put the date, sign, and print the addresses they live at. The person doing a Will is called the "Testator"

USUAL RESIDUE CLAUSE HAS 2 PLACES TO NAME PERSONS TO GET THINGS

In a Will "Residue Clause" anything left over after other Will parts is transferred as the clause directs. Many people use a Residue Clause to gift most their things. In this Will form's Residue Clause there is:

1) a 1st space to name 1 or more persons to get the Residue, and if any named here have died before the Will maker then other persons named here in this 1st space take the dead person's share, and

2) a 2nd space to name people to get things if all people named in the 1st space have died, and if any people named in the 2nd space have died their shares go to "lineal descendants" like their children.

People often put in the 1st space a spouse or closest family or friends, and in 2nd space next closest people.

TESTATOR AND 2 WITNESSES WHILE TOGETHER SIGN WILL

This Will after being filled out (except bits intentionally left blank) must be signed by the person doing the Will (the "Testator") in front of at least 2 persons acting as witnesses at least age 18 who then also sign.

LAST WILL AND TESTAMENT

I, _____, of _____, Maine, do revoke all prior Wills and testamentary documents and do make, publish, and declare this as my Will. I am of sound mind and under no duress or undue influence and acting voluntarily.

1. LIST OF SPOUSE AND CHILDREN. To help show I am mentally competent and have sufficient memory to make a Will I wish to list any living spouse and living children I now have. I currently have the following living spouse and living children:

_____
_____.

2. GIFTS. I give these gifts in this Will, but to get a gift in this section the recipient must survive me except as otherwise stated below.

I give _____ to _____.
I give _____ to _____.
I give _____ to _____.
I give _____ to _____.
I give _____ to _____.
I give _____ to _____.

3. SEPARATE WRITINGS. I may do writings separate from this Will to gift tangible personal property as allowed by state law, and all such writings should be followed. But any such writing not found within 90 days of my death is canceled and has no effect. A gift in such a writing to a person who does not survive me is canceled and has no effect. This Will does not revoke any such writings that now exist.

4. RESIDUE. I give the rest and residue and remainder of my estate, my money and property of any kind and nature, and anything I have an interest in so long as it was not transferred by other Will provisions (all of which is called the "residue"), as follows:
   a) to _____ who survive me with persons just named who survive me taking the share of non-survivors, then if anything remains
   b) to _____ and if any of those just named do not survive me their part goes to their lineal descendants per stirpes.

5. ADMINISTRATION. I name, nominate, and appoint _____ as Personal Representative including for me, my Will, and my estate.

6. GUARDIAN. I name, nominate, and appoint _____
to be Guardian of any minor child of mine and to have care, authority, custody, and other control of them. I also name this same person to be Conservator for any minor child and to have care, control, and power over their property, money, and estate.

7. MISCELLANEOUS. The following applies to this Will and generally.
   In this Will no part left unfilled is a mistake including spaces in the residue clause.
   The facts support and I want Maine state law to apply to this Will and my estate.
   I order that my just debts, funeral and related expenses, and taxes be paid as soon after my death as practical but only those items my Personal Representative chooses to pay.
   Priority of Will gifts of the same type is based on the order they are written.
   The words "give" and "gift" also means a devise, bequest, grant, legacy, or similar.
   I am intentionally not providing by Will or other ways for some family, including I am not providing for some children of mine and also children of a deceased child of mine.
   If a gift Will reasonably mentions survival then survival is an absolute condition and anti-lapse laws or similar provisions have no effect and without survival the gift lapses. Unless a Will gift specifies otherwise if a Will gift goes to multiple recipients if any do not survive me the part to them lapses and instead goes to other surviving recipients.
   No earlier money transfer reduces a Will gift unless I always called it a loan or similar.
   In this Will any gender or gendered word includes all genders, and the singular includes the plural and vice versa, and "they" can mean a single person or many persons.
   Unless a Will specifically says otherwise a secured debt including a mortgage or lien shall not be paid off including by a Personal Representative or in probate, and a recipient of a Will gift of property takes it subject to debts. Also, no recipient of property who may lose it or who pays to keep it may have my estate or others pay or do exoneration.
   If at death I no longer have an item in a specific gift the gift is void and extinguished.
   I request and authorize any informal, summary, and quick probate or similar action. Any Personal Representative may act independently with no supervision of any court, including independent administration, and with no inventory, appraisal, or other action.
   I give any Personal Representative the a) fullest authority, discretion, and powers allowed by state law, b) power to lease, sell, mortgage, convey, or keep property including real property in a manner and time they deem helpful or proper, and c) authority to settle or pay claims or debts in the time and manner they choose. Any Personal Representative or other fiduciary shall have all powers and authorities conferred by statute or common law in any jurisdiction they may act.
   Any Guardian of any type, Conservator, Custodian, or other person managing a minor's property or money may use or invade the principal and sell property without court action. A person named to manage things for a minor shall do this in similar roles outside Maine.
   If context permits the terms Personal Representative and Executor and Administrator are interchangeable, Conservator and Guardian of the Estate and Guardian of Property and

Custodian are interchangeable, and residue and residuary are interchangeable. Any such person may stand in the place of and have all powers like the others named here.

The residue includes lapsed or failed gifts, insurance paid to the estate, digital assets, inheritances owed me, and all I had power of appointment or testamentary disposition over.

Any Personal Representative may access, manage, delete, modify, transfer, and otherwise control any digital accounts and assets I had any interest in or power over.

Any Personal Representative, Executor, Administrator, Guardian of any type like for a person or estate, Conservator, Custodian, and any other fiduciary under this Will or otherwise shall qualify and serve without bond, surety, security, surety bond, or similar.

If evidence does not show it likely a person survived me by 120 hours (5 days) then for this Will and my estate they shall be deemed in all ways as having died before me.

If part of this Will is by law invalid or unenforceable other provisions remain in effect.

Any Personal Representative may at any time transfer money or property of a minor under age 18 to a Custodian to serve under the Maine Uniform Transfers to Minors Act or similar law anywhere, and may pick a person to be Custodian including themselves.

TESTATOR

IN WITNESS WHEREOF, I declare and publish that this instrument is my Will which I make as Testator, that I do this as a free and voluntary act for the purposes expressed therein, that I am at least 18 years of age and of sound mind and under no constraint or undue influence, and I do sign this instrument voluntarily as my Will in the presence and sight of each of the persons acting as witnesses who are named and who sign below, this _____ day of _____, 20___ .

_____
Testator signature

WITNESSES

We, the persons signing below, declare that in the presence and sight of each of us persons that _____ as Testator did voluntarily publish, declare, and sign the foregoing instrument as the Will of the Testator, that to the best of our knowledge the Testator is at least 18 years of age and of sound mind and under no constraint or undue influence, that each of us persons who sign below is at least 18 years old and fully competent to act as witnesses, and that in the presence and sight of Testator and each other we sign our names to witness this Will at the Testator's request.

_____   _____
Signature of Witness #1   Address of Witness #1

_____   _____
Signature of Witness #2   Address of Witness #2

CHAPTER 9
FORM 3: MAINE STATUTORY WILL

FORM IS A WILL FOUND IN LAW THAT'S SIMPLE BUT INFLEXIBLE

The "Maine Statutory Will" was put into state law (the statutes) by the legislature for people to use if they want, and it is simple but inflexible, and people using often <u>are less wealthy or want to save time</u>.

WILL HAS PARTS TO ALLOW SOME GIFTS BUT IS NOT FLEXIBLE

First, the form handles <u>real property</u> (land and building) and says gifts of this can be done by writing them here, and then says real property not gifted goes first to any living spouse and then to any surviving children.

Second, the form handles <u>personal and household items</u> next ("furniture, furnishings, household items, autos, and personal items") and says gifts of this can be done by writing them here, and then says any such property not gifted goes first to any living spouse and then to any surviving children.

Third, next the form handles cash gifts to charities, institutions, and government agencies and says these can be written in here.

Fourth, the form next handles any property and money left, often called the "residue" and the form calls "All other Assets (My "Residuary Estate")". The form lets a person initial 1 of 3 boxes to pick (pick only 1):

A: all to living spouse or if none then it is split among living children and descendants of any dead child,
B: lets dollar amount be written to go to living spouse and rest is split among living children and descendants of any dead child,
C: lets dollar amounts be written to go to multiple persons named.

<u>Most people pick option A so any living spouse gets it but if there is none then a person's children gets it</u>.

The last area, "Undistributed Property", has place to write persons to get things if somehow anything is left. All people must sign at the Residue paragraph end at the line saying "this paragraph only valid if signed".

WILL THEN CAN NAME PERSONS TO DO JOBS

The Will then has areas to name people to do jobs. There is spot to name a "Personal Representative" to handle things after death, name a "Guardian" to care for minor child under 18, and name a "Conservator" to manage a minor child's money and property. Most people name 1 person for many jobs. People can skip naming someone for a job if they won't need it (like if they have no small child). In the form after naming a person a signature is needed. But this form has no easy way to say no bond (insurance) will be needed later by people when they serve, and due to this some people do not use this form.

COMPLETE WILL BY SIGNING WITH 2 WITNESSES

This form is a statutory form found in Maine law and this book's form is copied from the version found on the Cumberland County website. *See www.cumberlandcountyme.gov.* People should print out this book's form and fill it in with pen or pencil. The form's end must be signed by a person with 2 witnesses who then sign too. The form has a spot for a 3rd witness which is optional. Any person at least 18 can be a witness. In the form are many other places to sign. <u>See the Appendix for a helpful example of how to fill out the form</u>. The last page is a "Self-Proving Affidavit" which as this book covers elsewhere is optional and needs a notary.

Maine Statutory Will

NOTICE TO THE PERSON WHO SIGNS THIS WILL:

1. THIS STATUTORY WILL HAS SERIOUS LEGAL EFFECTS ON YOUR FAMILY AND PROPERTY. IF THERE IS ANYTHING IN THIS WILL THAT YOU DO NOT UNDERSTAND, YOU SHOULD CONSULT A LAWYER AND ASK THE LAWYER TO EXPLAIN IT TO YOU.

2. THIS WILL DOES NOT DISPOSE OF PROPERTY THAT PASSES ON YOUR DEATH TO ANY PERSON BY OPERATION OF LAW OR BY CONTRACT. FOR EXAMPLE, THE WILL DOES NOT DISPOSE OF JOINT TENANCY ASSETS OR YOUR SPOUSE'S ELECTIVE SHARE, AND IT WILL NOT NORMALLY APPLY TO PROCEEDS OF LIFE INSURANCE ON YOUR LIFE OR YOUR RETIREMENT PLAN BENEFITS.

3. THIS WILL IS NOT DESIGNED TO REDUCE DEATH TAXES OR ANY OTHER TAXES. YOU SHOULD DISCUSS THE TAX RESULTS OF YOUR DECISIONS WITH A COMPETENT TAX ADVISOR.

4. YOU CANNOT CHANGE, DELETE, OR ADD WORDS TO THE FACE OF THIS MAINE STATUTORY WILL. YOU SHOULD MARK THROUGH ALL SECTIONS OR PARTS OF SECTIONS THAT YOU DO NOT COMPLETE. YOU MAY REVOKE THIS MAINE STATUTORY WILL AND YOU MAY AMEND IT BY CODICIL.

5. THIS WILL TREATS ADOPTED CHILDREN AS IF THEY ARE NATURAL CHILDREN.

6. IF YOU MARRY OR DIVORCE AFTER YOU SIGN THIS WILL, YOU SHOULD MAKE AND SIGN A NEW WILL.

7. IF YOU HAVE ANOTHER CHILD AFTER YOU SIGN THIS WILL, YOU SHOULD MAKE AND SIGN A NEW WILL.

8. THIS WILL IS NOT VALID UNLESS IT IS SIGNED BY AT LEAST TWO WITNESSES. YOU SHOULD CAREFULLY READ AND FOLLOW THE WITNESSING PROCEDURE DESCRIBED AT THE END OF THIS WILL.

9. YOU SHOULD KEEP THIS WILL IN YOUR SAFE-DEPOSIT BOX OR OTHER SAFE PLACE.

10. IF YOU HAVE ANY DOUBTS WHETHER OR NOT THIS WILL ADEQUATELY SETS OUT YOUR WISHES FOR THE DISPOSITION OF YOUR PROPERTY, YOU SHOULD CONSULT A LAWYER.

Maine Statutory Will of

_____
(Print your name)

Article 1. Declaration

This is my will and I revoke any prior wills and codicils.

Article 2. Disposition of my property

2.1 REAL PROPERTY. I give all my real property to my spouse, if living; otherwise it shall be equally divided among my children who survive me; except as specifically provided below: (specific distribution not valid without signature.)

    I leave the following specific real property to the person(s) named:

(name)	(description of item)	(signature)
_____	_____	_____
_____	_____	_____
_____	_____	_____
_____	_____	_____
_____	_____	_____

2.2 PERSONAL AND HOUSEHOLD ITEMS. I give all my furniture, furnishings, household items, personal automobiles and personal items to my spouse, if living; otherwise they shall be equally divided among my children who survive me; except as specifically provided below: (specific distribution not valid without signature.)

    I leave the following specific items to the person(s) named:

(name)	(description of item)	(signature)
_____	_____	_____
_____	_____	_____
_____	_____	_____
_____	_____	_____
_____	_____	_____

2.3 CASH GIFT TO CHARITABLE ORGANIZATIONS OR INSTITUTIONS: I make the following cash gift(s) to the named charitable organizations or institutions in the amount stated. If I fail to sign this provision, no gift is made. If the charitable organization or institution does not survive me or accept the gift, then no gift is made.

(name)	(amount)	(signature)
_____	_____	_____
_____	_____	_____
_____	_____	_____

2.4 ALL OTHER ASSETS (MY "RESIDUARY ESTATE"). I adopt only one Property Disposition Clause by placing my initials in the box in front of the letter "A", "B" or "C" signifying which clause I wish to adopt. I place my signature after clause "A" or clause "B", or after each individual distribution in clause "C". If I fail to sign the appropriate distribution(s) or if I sign in more than one clause or if I fail to place my initials in the appropriate box, this paragraph 2.4 will be invalid and I realize that the remainder of my property will be distributed as if I did not make a will.

Property Disposition Clauses. (Select one.)

☐ A. I leave all my remaining property to my spouse, if living. If my spouse is not living, then in equal shares to my children and the descendents of any deceased child.

_____
(signature)

☐ B. I leave the following stated amount to my spouse _____ and the remainder in equal shares to my children and the descendents of any deceased child. If my spouse is not living, that share shall be distributed in equal shares to my children and the descendents of any deceased child.

_____
(signature)

☐ C. I leave the following stated amounts to the persons named:

(name)	(amount)	(signature)
_____	_____	_____
_____	_____	_____
_____	_____	_____
_____	_____	_____
_____	_____	_____

2.5 UNDISTRIBUTED PROPERTY. If I have any property that, for any reason, does not pass under the other parts of this will, all of that property shall be distributed as follows: (Draw a line through any unused space.)

_____
(this paragraph only valid if signed)

Article 3. Nomination of guardian, conservator and personal representative

3.1 GUARDIAN. (if you have a child under 18 years of age, you may name at least one person to serve as guardian for the child.)

If a guardian is needed for any child of mine, then I nominate the first guardian named below to serve as guardian of that child. If the person does not serve, then the others shall serve in the order I list them. My nomination of a guardian is not valid without my signature.

FIRST GUARDIAN _____ _____
(signature)

SECOND GUARDIAN _____ _____
(signature)

THIRD GUARDIAN _____ _____
(signature)

3.2 CONSERVATOR. (A conservator may be named to manage the property of a minor child. You do not need to name a conservator if you wish the guardian to act as conservator. If you wish to name a conservator in addition to a guardian, complete this paragraph, 3.2. If you do not wish to name a separate conservator, do not complete this paragraph.)

I nominate the first conservator named below to serve as conservator for any minor children of mine. If the first conservator does not serve, then the others shall serve in the order I list them. My nomination of a conservator is not valid without my signature.

FIRST CONSERVATOR _____ _____
(signature)

SECOND CONSERVATOR _____ _____
(signature)

THIRD CONSERVATOR _____ _____
(signature)

3.3 PERSONAL REPRESENTATIVE. (Name at least one.) I nominate the person or institution named as first personal representative below to administer the provisions of this will. If that person or institution does not serve, then I nominate the others to serve in the order I list them. My nomination of a personal representative is not valid without my signature.

FIRST PERSONAL
REPRESENTATIVE_____   _____
                                                                                              (signature)

SECOND PERSONAL
REPRESENTATIVE_____   _____
                                                                                              (signature)

THIRD PERSONAL
REPRESENTATIVE_____   _____
                                                                                              (signature)

I sign my name to this Maine Statutory Will on _____ at _____
                                                                                (date)   (city)
in the State of _____.

_____
Your Signature

STATEMENT OF WITNESSES (You must have two witnesses.)

    Each of us declares that the person who signed above willingly signed this Maine Statutory Will in our presence or willingly directed another to sign it for him or her or that he or she acknowledged that the signature on this Maine Statutory Will is his or hers or that he or she acknowledged that this Maine Statutory Will is his or her will and we sign below as witnesses to that signing.

Signature _____

Printed name _____

Address _____

Signature _____

Printed name _____

Address _____

SELF-PROVING AFFIDAVIT (OPTIONAL)

Notary or other authorized person (optional)

Completing the following section and having all signatures acknowledged by a notary pubic or other individual authorized to take acknowledgments is optional but if completed will simplify the submission of your will to the probate court after your death.

I,_____ , the testator, on this _____ day of _____ 20___, being first duly sworn, do hereby declare to the undersigned authority that I sign and execute this instrument as my last will and that I sign it willingly (or willingly direct another to sign for me) as my free and voluntary act and that I am 18 years of age or older or am a legally emancipated minor, of sound mind and under no constraint or undue influence.

_____
Testator

We, _____ and _____ the witnesses, being first duly sworn, do hereby declare to the undersigned authority that the testator has signed and executed this instrument as (his)(her) last will and that (he)(she) signed it willingly (or willingly directed another to sign for (him)(her)), and that each of us, in the presence and hearing of the testator, signs this will as witness to the testator's signing, and that to the best of our knowledge the testator is 18 years of age or older or is a legally emancipated minor, of sound mind and under no constraint or undue influence.

_____
Witness

_____
Witness

The State of _____

County of _____

Subscribed, sworn to and acknowledged before me by _____, the testator, and subscribed and sworn to before me by _____ and _____, witnesses, this _____ Day of _____, 20___.

(Signed)_____
    (Official capacity of officer)

CHAPTER 10
FORM 4: HANDWRITTEN WILL

WILL CAN SKIP USING THE NORMAL 2 WITNESSES IF IT'S HANDWRITTEN

A Handwritten Will is a Will that is easier to do since it does not need the usual 2 witnesses if it is all handwritten by the person doing the Will.

HANDWRITTEN WILL WITHOUT WITNESSES IS ALLOWED IN MAINE

In 27 states including Maine a person doing a Will can skip using the usual 2 witnesses for a Will if: 1) it is all handwritten by the person doing the Will (not photocopied, typed, computer printed, or handwritten by anyone else), and 2) it is signed and dated. Many people call this a Handwritten Will and most lawyers call it a Holographic Will (holo means whole, and graph means image in the Greek language). These Wills are allowed since handwriting is harder to fake, people may be in an emergency or rush, witnesses may be scarce in the countryside, it is private, it can be cheap by skipping complexity and people, and it is traditional to allow this especially in rural places. The 27 states with Handwritten Wills have 55% of the U.S. population. See states with Handwritten Wills on map below in dark.

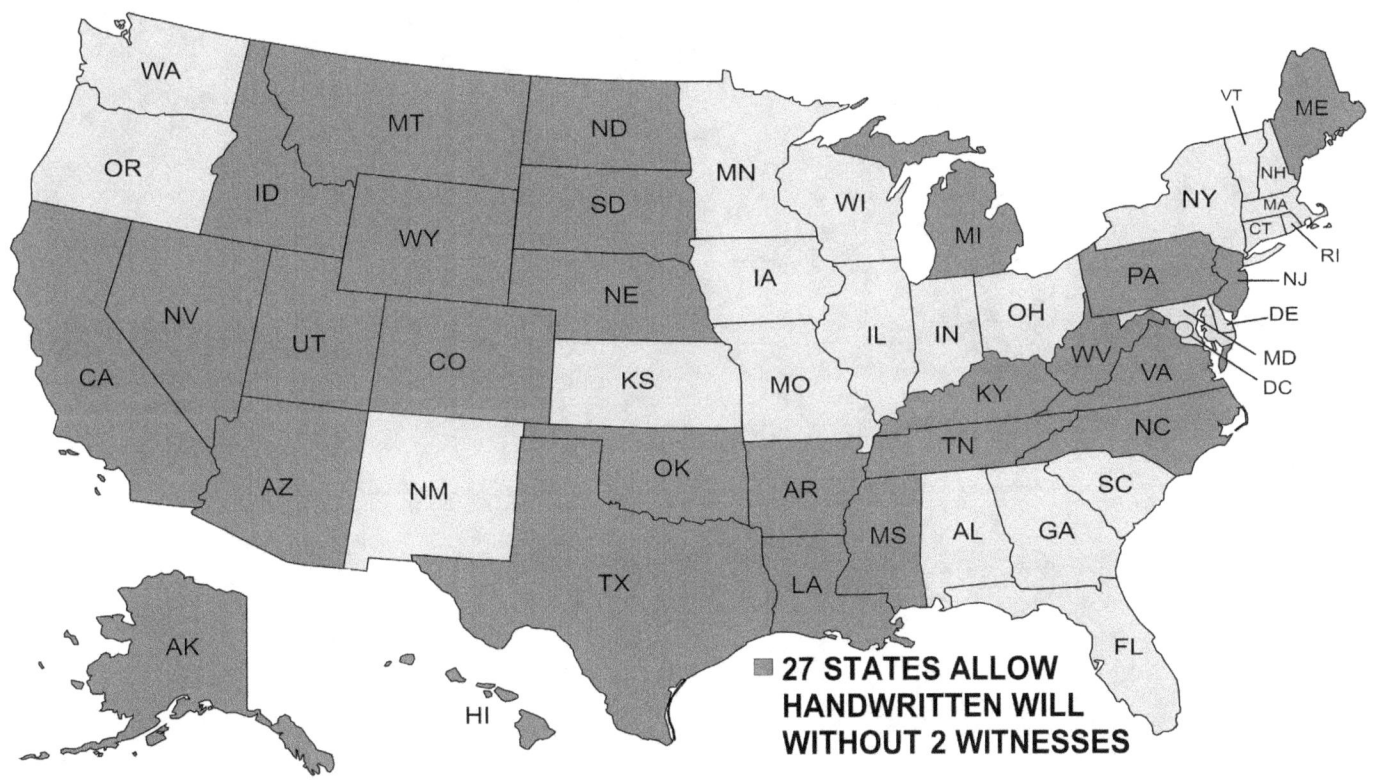

HANDWRITTEN WILLS ARE USUALLY FINE BUT REQUIRE LATER WORK

Some lawyers warn against Handwritten Wills saying they often read confusingly, skip legal words that help in some cases, and are found invalid more often – but some studies show they are liked and usually fine. To use a Handwritten Will later after a death some people must in writing or in testimony say the handwriting looks like the Testator's, which can be a hassle. But a normal Will if no Self-Proving Affidavit was done also needs similar proof like from a witness to the signing or other proof of signing. Handwritten Wills tend to be done by people who are young so unlikely to need a Will soon, who are in a hurry, who want to fix a mistake, who before a trip want to pick a Guardian, who moved to a new state, or who plan to do a better Will later.

WORDS BELOW ON THIS PAGE CAN BE USED FOR A HANDWRITTEN WILL

People can do a Handwritten Will in a sentence that is legal but may leave out helpful parts, for example: *"As my Will I give my estate and all else to Ann Baker who shall be Executor. - Dan Baker"* But it is recommended people use more complex words for a Handwritten Will shown on this page below. To do this people should change the names and words below on this page to match what they want done. If some people named to get things later die it is best to quickly re-do the Will and name different people. The last paragraph about Guardians for children can be skipped if a person has no children under age 18. This Will must be all handwritten by the person doing it on some paper (pencil is allowed) and then signed and dated by the person (usually in pen or permanent marker).

WILL

1. I am John Max Hill and I live in Cumberland County in Maine. I revoke any prior Wills and Codicils and declare this to be my Will.

2. I give my estate and all else to Jane Eve Hill and Wendy Sue Baker. My not giving to some other family of mine is intentional.

3. I name Jane Eve Hill as Personal Representative for me, my Will, and my estate.

4. No bond or similar is needed for any Personal Representative, Guardian, Conservator, or other person. I request informal probate.

5. If ever needed for a minor child I name Mary Jennifer Dodd as Guardian of the Person to have care, custody, and control of them. I name this same person as Conservator to have control and power over any minor child's property, money, and estate.

May 8, 2024   *John Max Hill*

CHAPTER 11
FORM 5: SELF-PROVING AFFIDAVIT

FORM CAN BE DONE TO MAKE USING A WILL LATER EASIER

This form is optional but can be done after a Will is done. This form helps when after a death people are trying to use a Will. This form is a statutory form found written in Maine law for people to find and use. This form can be used with the Wills in Form 1 and Form 2 in this book. Form 3 in this book, the Maine Statutory Will form, already has a Self-Proving Affidavit form on the last page for people to use if they want.

FORM SAVES LATER WORK OF SHOWING WILL WAS PROPERLY SIGNED

A Self-Proving Affidavit "proves" a Will was signed properly. If this form is not done then after death a little work is need to get evidence from either witnesses to the Will signing, persons familiar with the signatures of people, or a handwriting expert. If this form is not done there is a bit more legal risk a Will won't be followed later. But of people doing Wills about half skip a Self-Proving Affidavit mostly due to hassle of finding a notary on top of 2 witnesses each time a Will is done or re-done, and since it mostly just saves a little later work of people who are happy to do work to get what a Will gives them.

FORM IS DONE BY TESTATOR AND 2 WITNESSES SIGNING BEFORE NOTARY

For this form to be valid a person who is a notary (also called a "notary public") must see the Testator and 2 witnesses sign and then the notary notarizes it. A notary can be found and politely asked to help at a bank, insurance agent, government office, or by looking in a phonebook. A notary is likelier to help if a person is an existing customer. This form is often done a few minutes after a Will is signed but it can be done much later (even years later) when everyone can meet with a notary. This form can't legally be done before a Will is done. This form when done is often kept paper-clipped to the Will it supports.

SELF-PROVING AFFIDAVIT

(18-C Maine Revised Statutes § 2-503)

The State of Maine

County of _____

We, _____, _____ and

_____, the Testator and the Witnesses, respectively, whose names are signed to the attached or foregoing instrument, being first duly sworn, do hereby declare to the undersigned authority that the Testator signed and executed the instrument as their Will and that they had signed willingly, as their free and voluntary act, and that each of the Witnesses, in the presence and hearing of the Testator, signed the Will acting as a witness and that to the best of their knowledge the Testator was at that time 18 years of age or older or a legally emancipated minor, of sound mind and under no constraint or undue influence.

_____
Testator

_____
Witness

_____
Witness

Subscribed, sworn to and acknowledged before me by _____, the Testator, and subscribed and sworn to before me by _____ and _____, Witnesses, this ____ day of _____, 20___.

(Signed) _____

_____
(Official capacity of officer)

CHAPTER 12
FORM 6: TANGIBLE PERSONAL PROPERTY LIST

FORM LETS GIFTS OF PROPERTY BE EASILY ADDED

This form lets a person easily anytime add gifts of tangible personal property to occur after their death. This is sometimes called a "Memorandum". Usually a person must have done a Will already to do this.

FORM GIVES EASY QUICK WAY TO WRITE MORE GIFTS OF PROPERTY

This form lets a person easily write some more gifts of property to occur at their death without having to re-write a Will. To use this form a valid Will must say that it can be used, and all this book's Will forms say this. If this form and a Will gift the same item then by law the Will controls. If more than 1 of these forms gift the same item then the more recently done page controls. People can modify an existing form page if they write a new date and signature on it. Note, to help avoid delay this book's form says to ignore any of these forms not found within 90 days of a death. About half of U.S. states have a similar form.

It may help understanding to show the Maine law allowing this form, which in its main part says:

18C M.R.S. §2-512. Separate writing identifying devise of certain types of tangible personal property

[A] will may refer to a written statement or list to dispose of items of tangible personal property not otherwise specifically disposed of by the will, other than money.

To be admissible under this section as evidence of the intended disposition, the writing must be in the handwriting of the testator or be signed by the testator and must describe the items and the devisees with reasonable certainty.

The writing may be referred to as one to be in existence at the time of the testator's death; it may be prepared before or after the execution of the will; it may be altered by the testator after its preparation; and it may be a writing that has no significance apart from its effect upon the dispositions made by the will.

FORM CAN ONLY GIFT TANGIBLE PERSONAL PROPERTY

By law the form can only gift "tangible personal property". This means stuff that is <u>tangible</u> (touchable), so not accounts or moneys or investments related to papers, banks, or some entity like a corporation or partnership or trust. This also means property that is <u>personal property</u>, so not real property (land or buildings) and not fixtures (anything buried or tied to land). The form also can't gift money, whether coin or paper currency, even if it's antique or foreign money. <u>Most lawyers also recommend people not use the form to give items used in a trade or business</u>. Improper property written in the form is later just ignored. This form is often used to gift clothes, furniture, vehicles (including cars and trucks and boats), antiques, electronics, appliances, tools, building supplies, art, and jewelry.

TO COMPLETE THE FORM JUST SIGN AND DATE IT

To be valid the form just must be signed and usually dated. Often many pages of these forms are kept paper-clipped to a Will.

TANGIBLE PERSONAL PROPERTY LIST

In this writing are gifts of tangible personal property to occur at my death, but this writing if not found by someone within 90 days of my death is canceled.

I may do many pages of these writings which should all be seen as one document. If there are conflicts among such writings the provisions of the more recent writing will revoke the inconsistent provisions of a prior writing.

If a person getting a gift below does not survive me such gift is void and canceled.

DESCRIPTION OF PROPERTY   **NAME OF PERSONS TO GET PROPERTY**

_____ to _____
_____ to _____
_____ to _____
_____ to _____
_____ to _____
_____ to _____
_____ to _____
_____ to _____
_____ to _____
_____ to _____
_____ to _____
_____ to _____
_____ to _____
_____ to _____
_____ to _____
_____ to _____
_____ to _____
_____ to _____

DATE:_____   **SIGNED:**_____

CHAPTER 13
FORM 7: POWER OF ATTORNEY FOR HEALTH CARE

FORM CAN NAME HEALTH CARE AGENT AND GIVE INSTRUCTIONS

This form lets a person name someone to control health care if later needed and give many health care instructions. Many people do this form and skip other health care forms. Note, paramedics and others in a hurry usually won't read and follow this long form, but people can do shorter forms (see later in this book). The form is a statutory form is found in state law for people to use if wanted, but other similar forms exist. The form is often known as a "Health Care Directive". The form may seem complex but just has a few parts:

EXPLANATION (OF FORM)
PART 1: POWER OF ATTORNEY FOR HEALTH CARE
PART 2: INSTRUCTIONS FOR HEALTH CARE (INCLUDING END-OF-LIFE ISSUES)
PART 3: DONATION OF ORGANS AT DEATH (OPTIONAL)
PART 4: DESIGNATION OF PRIMARY PHYSICIAN (OPTIONAL)
MISCELLANEOUS AND SIGNATURES

FORM CAN NAME SOMEONE AS AGENT TO CONTROL HEALTH CARE

The form lets someone be named as "Agent" to have power to make medical decisions is ever needed (like if a person is later incapacitated by inability to stay conscious or be rational). Often named as Agent is a spouse, adult child, relative, or friend. The form has room to name additional persons to serve if needed but many people skip this. Naming family in the form can avoid their need to see a judge in an emergency.

IN FORM CAN GIVE END-OF-LIFE (LIVING WILL) INSTRUCTIONS

In the form a person can give instructions on stopping care if later doctors think more care won't help and a person is incapacitated. This is often called "Living Will" issues, or called "end-of-life" issues, and many states do this in a separate form. But many people skip these issues since this rarely matters, these things are stressful to decide, and people trust their Agent or family. This area also usually covers artificial nutrition (tube feeding) and also limiting pain with medications even if it may slightly shorten life.

IN FORM CAN GIVE INSTRUCTIONS AND COVER ORGAN DONATION

In the form a person can write health care instructions that any Agent, family, and doctors must all follow. But many people skip written instructions since they are hard to write to cover all situations, it can be stressful to decide health things, and people trust any Agent and family to make wise decisions if needed. Many people verbally tell family and friends their feelings about health. Many people skip parts of this form. The form can cover organ donation but most people do this in drivers license forms or state ID paperwork.

SIGN FORM WITH 2 WITNESSES

To complete the form a person signs and then 2 witnesses sign. Witnesses must be at least 18 and usually not a spouse or close family, not employees of a health care or insurance company involved in care, and not someone named Agent in the form. Once completed a person usually shows the form to any place that may give care to make it part of a person's medical file and followed. A person often hands the form to the Agent given power. To cancel the form a person usually tells all places that were shown the form.

POWER OF ATTORNEY FOR HEALTH CARE
(ADVANCE HEALTH CARE DIRECTIVE)

(18-C Maine Revised Statutes § 5-805)

Explanation

You have the right to give instructions about your own health care. You also have the right to name someone else to make health care decisions for you. This form lets you do either or both of these things. It also lets you express your wishes regarding donation of organs and the designation of your primary physician. If you use this form, you may complete or modify all or any part of it. You are free to use a different form.

Part 1 of this form is a power of attorney for health care. Part 1 lets you name another individual as agent to make health care decisions for you if you become incapable of making your own decisions or if you want someone else to make those decisions for you now even though you are still capable. You may also name an alternate agent to act for you if your first choice is not willing, able or reasonably available to make decisions for you. Unless related to you, your agent may not be an owner, operator or employee of a residential long-term health care institution at which you are receiving care.

Unless the form you sign limits the authority of your agent, your agent may make all health care decisions for you. This form has a place for you to limit the authority of your agent. You need not limit the authority of your agent if you wish to rely on your agent for all health care decisions that may have to be made. If you choose not to limit the authority of your agent, your agent will have the right to:

    (1) Consent or refuse consent to any care, treatment, service or procedure to maintain, diagnose or otherwise affect a physical or mental condition;
    (2) Select or discharge health care providers and institutions;
    (3) Approve or disapprove diagnostic tests, surgical procedures, programs of medication and orders not to resuscitate; and
    (4) Direct the provision, withholding or withdrawal of artificial nutrition and hydration and all other forms of health care, including life-sustaining treatment.

Part 2 of this form lets you give specific instructions about any aspect of your health care. Choices are provided for you to express your wishes regarding the provision, withholding or withdrawal of treatment to keep you alive, including the provision of artificial nutrition and hydration, as well as the provision of pain relief. Space is also provided for you to add to the choices you have made or for you to write out any additional wishes.

Part 3 of this form lets you express an intention to donate your bodily organs and tissues following your death.

Part 4 of this form lets you designate a physician to have primary responsibility for your health care.

After completing this form, sign and date the form at the end. You must have 2 other individuals sign as witnesses. Give a copy of the signed and completed form to your physician, to any other health care providers you may have, to any health care institution at which you are receiving care and to any health care agents you have named. You should talk to the person you have named as agent to make sure that he or she understands your wishes and is willing to take the responsibility.

You have the right to revoke this advance health care directive or replace this form at any time.

PART 1: POWER OF ATTORNEY FOR HEALTH CARE

(1) DESIGNATION OF AGENT: I _____ designate the following individual as my agent to make health care decisions for me:

_____
(name of individual you choose as agent)

_____
(address)   (city)   (state)   (zip code)

_____
(home phone)   (work phone)

OPTIONAL: If I revoke my agent's authority or if my agent is not willing, able or reasonably available to make a health care decision for me, I designate as my first alternate agent:

_____
(name of individual you choose as first alternate agent)

_____
(address)   (city)   (state)   (zip code)

_____
(home phone)   (work phone)

OPTIONAL: If I revoke the authority of my agent and first alternate agent or if neither is willing, able or reasonably available to make a health care decision for me, I designate as my second alternate agent:

_____
(name of individual you choose as second alternate agent)

_____
(address)   (city)   (state)   (zip code)

_____
(home phone)   (work phone)

(2) AGENT'S AUTHORITY: My agent is authorized to make all health care decisions for me, including decisions to provide, withhold or withdraw artificial nutrition and hydration and all other forms of health care to keep me alive, except as I state here:

_____
_____
_____
_____
_____

(Add additional sheets if needed.)

(3) WHEN AGENT'S AUTHORITY BECOMES EFFECTIVE: My agent's authority becomes effective when my primary physician determines that I am unable to make my own health care decisions unless I mark the following box. If I mark this box [   ], my agent's authority to make health care decisions for me takes effect immediately.

(4) AGENT'S OBLIGATION: My agent shall make health care decisions for me in accordance with this power of attorney for health care, any instructions I give in Part 2 of this form and my other wishes to the extent known to my agent. To the extent my wishes are unknown, my agent shall make health care decisions for me in accordance with what my agent determines to be in my best interest. In determining my best interest, my agent shall consider my personal values to the extent known to my agent.

(5) NOMINATION OF GUARDIAN: If a guardian of my person needs to be appointed for me by a court, I nominate the agent designated in this form. If that agent is not willing, able or reasonably available to act as guardian, I nominate the alternate agents whom I have named, in the order designated.

PART 2: INSTRUCTIONS FOR HEALTH CARE

If you are satisfied to allow your agent to determine what is best for you in making end-of-life decisions, you need not fill out this part of the form. If you do fill out this part of the form, you may strike any wording you do not want.

(6) END-OF-LIFE DECISIONS: I direct that my health care providers and others involved in my care provide, withhold or withdraw treatment in accordance with the choice I have marked below:

[   ] **(a) Choice Not To Prolong Life:** I do not want my life to be prolonged if (i) I have an incurable and irreversible condition that will result in my death within a relatively short time, (ii) I become unconscious and, to a reasonable degree of medical certainty, I will not regain consciousness or (iii) the likely risks and burdens of treatment would outweigh the expected benefits, **OR**

[   ] **(b) Choice To Prolong Life:** I want my life to be prolonged as long as possible within the limits of generally accepted health care standards.

(7) ARTIFICIAL NUTRITION AND HYDRATION: Artificial nutrition and hydration must be provided, withheld or withdrawn in accordance with the choice I have made in paragraph (6) unless I mark the following box. If I mark this box **[   ]**, artificial nutrition and hydration must be provided regardless of my condition and regardless of the choice I have made in paragraph (6).

(8) RELIEF FROM PAIN: Except as I state in the following space, I direct that treatment for alleviation of pain or discomfort be provided at all times, even if it hastens my death:

_____
_____

(9) OTHER WISHES: (If you do not agree with any of the optional choices above and wish to write your own, or if you wish to add to the instructions you have given above, you may do so here.) I direct that:

_____
_____
_____

(Add additional sheets if needed)

PART 3: DONATION OF ORGANS AT DEATH (OPTIONAL)

(10) UPON MY DEATH: (mark applicable box)

[ ] (a) I give any needed organs, tissues or parts, OR
[ ] (b) I give the following organs, tissues or parts only:_____
[ ] (c) My gift is for the following purposes: (strike any of the following you don't want)
    (i) Transplant   (ii) Therapy   (iii) Research   (iv) Education

PART 4: DESIGNATION OF PRIMARY PHYSICIAN (OPTIONAL)

(11) DESIGNATION: I designate the following physician as my primary physician:

_____
(name of physician)   (phone)

_____
(address)   (city)   (state)   (zip code)

OPTIONAL: If the physician I have designated above is not willing, able or reasonably available to act as my primary physician, I designate the following physician as my primary physician:

_____
(name of physician)   (phone)

_____
(address)   (city)   (state)   (zip code)

(12) EFFECT OF COPY: A copy of this form has the same effect as the original.

(13) SIGNATURES: Sign and date the form here:

_____
(sign your name)   (date)

_____
(print your name)   (phone)

_____
(address)   (city)   (state)   (zip code)

SIGNATURES OF WITNESSES:
Witness 1:

_____
(sign your name)   (date)   (print your name)

_____
(address)   (city)   (state)   (zip code)

Witness 2:

_____
(sign your name)   (date)   (print your name)

_____
(address)   (city)   (state)   (zip code)

CHAPTER 14
FORM 8: DO NOT RESUSCITATE

IN FORM CAN IMMEDIATELY REFUSE MOST HEALTH CARE

This chapter actually has 2 forms which are similar and people pick from to do the serious act of saying to immediately no longer try certain or most health care. Doing this is serious and often only the sickest or oldest people do it. Both forms are often called the "Do Not Resuscitate" or "DNR" form. Both forms are official state forms. Both forms are short and usually will be followed by paramedics and similar personnel.

FIRST FORM SAYS TO IMMEDIATELY NOT TRY MANY KINDS OF CARE

This chapter's first form, the Physician Orders For Life-Sustaining Treatment (the "P.O.L.S.T." form), says to immediately not try the many kinds of health care chosen in the form. This form often says to immediately no longer try antibiotics, artificial feeding, and C.P.R. This form is short so it can be read fast and be followed by those in a hurry like paramedics outside a health facility, but this P.O.L.S.T. form is more often used by people who are in a care facility. Pain relief and comfort care is usually still given, so paramedics are still usually called if needed. After doing this form a person is usually free to verbally override it, like by saying a person changed their mind and now do want care to a paramedic or doctor. In recent years the P.O.L.S.T. form has become the usual form used to say to immediately no longer try certain health care, and other forms are less often used including this chapter's second form.

SECOND FORM SAYS TO IMMEDIATELY NOT TRY RESUSCITATION

This chapter's second form, the Do-Not-Resuscitate Directive form says to immediately not provide resuscitation, which is trying to restart or help breathing or the heart. Resuscitation covers cardio-pulmonary resuscitation (C.P.R.), defibrillation (electric shocks), and machine or tube breathing. This form is short so it can be read fast and followed by those in a hurry like paramedics, and this Do-Not-Resuscitate Directive form is more often used by people outside and not inside a care facility. Pain relief and comfort care is usually still given, so paramedics are still usually called if needed. Note, even after doing form a person is usually free to verbally override it, like by saying to a paramedic or doctor to give all care. Some people also choose to wear a special DNR bracelet made by companies chosen by the state that doctors can help order.

FORM IS SIGNED BY DOCTOR OR SIMILAR AND THEN THE PATIENT

To be valid form these forms must be signed by a person's doctor (physician) or other similar health professional, and by the person doing the form (or their named representative who is authorized to do this). Once the form is done people usually people show it to all places that may give care to add it medical files so it is followed. Usually the person also keeps a copy of the form near their body to show to paramedics or similar personnel who may try to give health care.

HIPAA PERMITS DISCLOSURE OF POLST ORDERS TO HEALTH CARE PROVIDERS AS NECESSARY FOR TREATMENT
SEND FORM WITH PATIENT WHENEVER TRANSFERRED OR DISCHARGED

Medical Record # (Optional)

Maine POLST Form: A Portable Medical Order

Health care providers should complete this form only after a conversation with their patient or the patient's representative. The POLST decision-making process is for patients who are at risk for a life-threatening clinical event because they have a serious life-limiting medical condition, which may include advanced frailty (www.polst.org/guidance-appropriate-patients-pdf).

Patient Information.   **Having a POLST form is always voluntary.**

This is a medical order, not an advance directive. For information about POLST and to understand this document, visit: www.polst.org/form

Patient First Name: _____
Middle Name/Initial: _____ Preferred name: _____
Last Name: _____ Suffix (Jr, Sr, etc): _____
DOB (mm/dd/yyyy): ___/___/___ State where form was completed: _____
Gender: ☐ M ☐ F ☐ X   Social Security Number's last 4 digits (optional): xxx-xx-___

A. Cardiopulmonary Resuscitation Orders. Follow these orders if patient has no pulse and is not breathing.

Pick 1

☐ **YES CPR: Attempt Resuscitation, including mechanical ventilation, defibrillation and cardioversion.** (Requires choosing Full Treatments in Section B)

☐ **NO CPR: Do Not Attempt Resuscitation.** (May choose any option in Section B)

B. Initial Treatment Orders. Follow these orders if patient has a pulse and/or is breathing.

Reassess and discuss interventions with patient or patient representative regularly to ensure treatments are meeting patient's care goals. Consider a time-trial of interventions based on goals and specific outcomes.

Pick 1

☐ **Full Treatments (required if choose CPR in Section A).** Goal: Attempt to sustain life by all medically effective means. Provide appropriate medical and surgical treatments as indicated to attempt to prolong life, including intensive care.

☐ **Selective Treatments.** Goal: Attempt to restore function while avoiding intensive care and resuscitation efforts (ventilator, defibrillation and cardioversion). May use non-invasive positive airway pressure, antibiotics and IV fluids as indicated. Avoid intensive care. Transfer to hospital if treatment needs cannot be met in current location.

☐ **Comfort-focused Treatments.** Goal: Maximize comfort through symptom management; allow natural death. Use oxygen, suction and manual treatment of airway obstruction as needed for comfort. Avoid treatments listed in full or select treatments unless consistent with comfort goal. Transfer to hospital **only** if comfort cannot be achieved in current setting.

C. Additional Orders or Instructions. These orders are in addition to those above (e.g., blood products, dialysis).
[EMS protocols may limit emergency responder ability to act on orders in this section.]

_____

D. Medically Assisted Nutrition (Offer food by mouth if desired by patient, safe and tolerated)

Pick 1

☐ Provide feeding through new or existing surgically-placed tubes
☐ Trial period for artificial nutrition but no surgically-placed tubes
☐ No artificial means of nutrition desired
☐ Discussed but no decision made (standard of care provided)

E. SIGNATURE: Patient or Patient Representative (eSigned documents are valid)

I understand this form is voluntary. I have discussed my treatment options and goals of care with my provider. If signing as the patient's representative, the treatments are consistent with the patient's known wishes and in their best interest.

✖ (required) _____

If other than patient, print full name: _____

Authority: _____

The most recently completed valid POLST form supersedes all previously completed POLST forms.

F. SIGNATURE: Health Care Provider (eSigned documents are valid)   Verbal orders are acceptable with follow up signature.

I have discussed this order with the patient or his/her representative. The orders reflect the patient's known wishes, to the best of my knowledge. [Note: Only licensed health care providers authorized by law to sign POLST form in state where completed may sign this order]

✖ (required) _____

Date (mm/dd/yyyy): Required ___/___/___
Phone #: (___) ___

Printed Full Name: _____
License/Cert. #: _____

Supervising physician signature: _____ ☐ N/A
License #: _____

A copied, faxed or electronic version of this form is a legal and valid medical order. This form does not expire.   2019

Maine POLST Form – Page 2   *****ATTACH TO PAGE 1*******

Patient Full Name:

Contact Information (Optional but helpful)

Patient's Emergency Contact. (Note: Listing a person here does **not** grant them authority to be a legal representative. Only an advance directive or state law can grant that authority.)

Full Name:	☐ Legal Representative ☐ Other emergency contact	Phone #: Day: ( ) Night: ( )

Primary Care Provider Name: | Phone: (   )

☐ Patient is enrolled in hospice | Name of Agency:
Agency Phone: (   )

Form Completion Information (Optional but helpful)

Reviewed patient's advance directive to confirm no conflict with POLST orders:
(A POLST form does not replace an advance directive or living will)

- ☐ Yes; date of the document reviewed: _____
- ☐ Conflict exists, notified patient (if patient lacks capacity, noted in chart)
- ☐ Advance directive not available
- ☐ No advance directive exists

Check everyone who participated in discussion:
☐ Patient with decision-making capacity ☐ Court Appointed Guardian ☐ Parent of Minor
☐ Legal Surrogate / Health Care Agent ☐ Other: _____

Professional Assisting Health Care Provider w/ Form Completion (if applicable):
Full Name: | Date (mm/dd/yyyy): / / | Phone #: (   )

This individual is the patient's: ☐ Social Worker ☐ Nurse ☐ Clergy ☐ Other:

Form Information & Instructions

- **Completing a POLST form:**
  - Provider should document basis for this form in the patient's medical record notes.
  - Patient representative is determined by applicable state law and, in accordance with state law, may be able to execute or to void this POLST form only if the patient lacks decision-making capacity.
  - Only licensed health care providers authorized to sign POLST forms in their state or D.C. can sign this form. See www.polst.org/state-signature-requirements-pdf for who is authorized in each state and D.C.
  - Original (if available) is given to patient; provider keeps a copy in medical record.
  - Last 4 digits of SSN are optional but can help identify / match a patient to their form.
  - If a translated POLST form is used during conversation, attach the translation to the signed English form.
- **Using a POLST form:**
  - Any incomplete section of POLST creates no presumption about patient's preferences for treatment. Provide standard of care.
  - No defibrillator (including automated external defibrillators) or chest compressions should be used if "No CPR" is chosen.
  - For all options, use medication by any appropriate route, positioning, wound care and other measures to relieve pain and suffering.
- **Reviewing a POLST form:** This form does not expire but should be reviewed whenever the patient:
  (1) is transferred from one care setting or level to another;
  (2) has a substantial change in health status;
  (3) changes primary provider; or
  (4) changes his/her treatment preferences or goals of care.
- **Modifying a POLST form:** This form cannot be modified. If changes are needed, void form and complete a new POLST form.
- **Voiding a POLST form:**
  - **If a patient or patient representative (for patients lacking capacity) wants to void the form**: destroy paper form and contact patient's health care provider to void orders in patient's medical record (and POLST registry, if applicable). State law may limit patient representative authority to void.
  - **For health care providers**: destroy patient copy (if possible), note in patient record form is voided and notify registries (if applicable).
- **Additional Forms.** Can be obtained by going to www.polst.org/form
- As permitted by law, this form may be added to a secure electronic registry so health care providers can find it.

State Specific Info	For Barcodes / ID Sticker

For more information, visit www.polst.org or email info@polst.org   Copied, faxed or electronic versions of this form are legal and valid.   2019

- - THIS PAGE INTENTIONALLY BLANK - -

DO-NOT-RESUSCITATE (DNR) DIRECTIVE

This section is optional. If you do not want ambulance crews to revive you if your heart or breathing stops, you **and** your physician (**or** nurse practitioner **or** physician assistant) must complete and sign this form.

FOR PATIENT TO COMPLETE after consultation with his or her health care provider:

In the event that my heart or breathing stops and I am unable to speak for myself, I, _____ (printed name) direct that no efforts be taken to restart my heart or breathing and that Emergency Medical Services (ambulance crews) if notified, honor my directive. I have come to this decision after considering my condition and prognosis and the potential risks, burdens and benefits of refusing efforts to restart my heart or breathing.

I understand that I may change my mind at any time by destroying this form and removing any Maine EMS approved Do-Not-Resuscitate jewelry, such as MedicAlert. I will also tell my physician (**or** nurse practitioner **or** physician assistant) and other caregivers if I change my mind.

I understand that this form is not valid until my physician (**or** nurse practitioner **or** physician assistant) **and** I have signed it.

I understand that in a hospital, nursing home, hospice or home health setting, federal law requires that my physician must include a specific DNR order in my medical record or plan of care, even if we have both signed this form.

☐ No expiration date **OR** ☐ Expires on _____

_____   _____
Patient Signature   Date Signed

FOR PHYSICIAN, PHYSICIAN ASSISTANT OR NURSE PRACTITIONER TO COMPLETE:

By my signature I affirm that:

(i) After meeting with this patient and discussing this decision, I am satisfied that the patient understands the potential risks, burdens and benefits of refusing resuscitative interventions in light of the patient's medical condition; and (ii) I believe that the patient has made a voluntary informed decision about resuscitation and I agree to comply with that decision. I will tell any health care providers providing care under my authority to comply with this decision.

_____   _____
Signature and license level (MD, DO, PA or NP)   Date Signed

_____   _____
Printed Name   Telephone Number

THIS FORM IS ENDORSED BY MAINE EMERGENCY MEDICAL SERVICES

Revised February 2008

CHAPTER 15
FORM 9: DURABLE POWER OF ATTORNEY

FORM LETS POWER BE GIVEN OVER PROPERTY, MONEY, AND MORE

This form lets a person give power to let someone do things with the person's money, property, debt, and more. There is no standard Maine form for this. Many people call this form a "Financial Power Of Attorney".

FORM GIVES POWER TO LET SOMEONE HELP WITH PROPERTY AND MONEY

This form lets a person (called in the form the "Principal") give power to someone (who is called in the form the "Agent" or "Attorney-in-Fact") to do things with the person's money and property and other things. Doing this form can let the Agent help and do chores, pay bills, move money in accounts, buy or sell items, sign contracts, take out debt, and get information from banks and others. This can help if a person is sick, busy, or away, and may avoid need for nursing home, conservator, or guardian. Often Agent is a trusted person like spouse, relative, or friend. A person until incapacitated like by illness can still make decisions and overrule or fire Agent. Some people modify form to give instructions or limit power but if it's unclear banks or others may be worried and not follow form. The form is called "durable" since it continues even if person is incapacitated, and is "general" since it is broad. If an Agent signs any document the signature should be like, "Mark Alan Smith signing as Agent under Power of Attorney for Mary Ann Polk".

DUE TO RISKS MANY SKIP THIS FORM OR CONSULT A LAWYER

Many people skip this form or first see a lawyer. Using this form is risky and can lead to harm since the Agent can be wasteful with money, commit fraud or theft, or by carelessness allow some other harms. A person acting as Agent has a duty to be loyal and act reasonably and can be sued for improper actions, but they may later be out of money to pay. Usually banks and others can't be blamed for obeying an Agent. The law is complex and basic acts of an Agent may be fine like paying bills, but some acts may be improper like making gifts, risky investments, or unusual acts. It is best a person not the Agent does anything unusual.

IT MAY BE IMPROPER FOR AGENT TO MAKE GIFTS OR DO OTHER THINGS

This area of law is complex and <u>basic acts may be fine</u> like paying bills, moving funds, requesting records, or signing contracts that help Principal. But <u>less usual acts may be improper</u> like as gift handing money or property to family or friends if large like over $1,000, making risky investment decisions, or doing anything unusual. Due to complex laws using the form can be risky and some people ask lawyer for advice.

SIGN FORM BEFORE NOTARY OR TWO WITNESSES

The form must be signed by a person while in front of someone who is a notary who then notarizes it. Most banks, financial companies, and insurance companies will not follow a form that is not notarized. The first page of the form is a "Notice" page that should be kept attached or kept close to rest of form. Once signed the form can be kept till needed or handed out immediately to person named Agent to hold. To cancel the form a person can take back copies, rip it up, mark it "void', and tell places that saw the form that it is cancelled.

NOTICE FOR DURABLE POWER OF ATTORNEY

Notice to the Principal: As the "Principal" you are using this power of attorney to grant power to another person (called the Agent) to make decisions about your property and to use your property on your behalf. Under this power of attorney you give your Agent broad and sweeping powers to sell or otherwise dispose of your property without notice to you. Under this document your Agent will continue to have these powers after you become incapacitated. The powers that you give your Agent are explained more fully in the Maine Uniform Power of Attorney Act, Maine Revised Statutes, <u>Title 18-C, Article 5, Part 9</u>. You have the right to revoke this power of attorney at any time as long as you are not incapacitated. If there is anything about this power of attorney that you do not understand, you should ask an attorney to explain it to you.

Notice to the Agent: As the "Agent" you are given power under this power of attorney to make decisions about the property belonging to the Principal and to dispose of the Principal's property on the Principal's behalf in accordance with the terms of this power of attorney. This power of attorney is valid only if the Principal is of sound mind when the Principal signs it. When you accept the authority granted under this power of attorney, a special legal relationship is created between you and the Principal. This relationship imposes upon you legal duties that continue until you resign or the power of attorney is terminated or revoked. The duties are more fully explained in the Maine Uniform Power of Attorney Act, Maine Revised Statutes, <u>Title 18-C, Article 5, Part 9</u> and <u>Title 18-B, sections 802</u> to <u>807</u> and <u>Title 18-B, chapter 9</u>. As the Agent, you are generally not entitled to use the Principal's property for your own benefit or to make gifts to yourself or others unless the power of attorney gives you such authority. If you violate your duty under this power of attorney, you may be liable for damages and may be subject to criminal prosecution. You must stop acting on behalf of the Principal if you learn of any event that terminates this power of attorney or your authority under this power of attorney. Events of termination are more fully explained in the Maine Uniform Power of Attorney Act and include, but are not limited to, revocation of your authority or of the power of attorney by the Principal, the death of the Principal or the commencement of divorce proceedings between you and the Principal. If there is anything about this power of attorney or your duties under it that you do not understand, you should ask an attorney to explain it to you

DURABLE POWER OF ATTORNEY

I _____ (insert name and address) appoint _____
_____ (insert the name and address of the person appointed) as my agent (attorney-in-fact) to act for me in any way including in any way which I myself could do if I were personally present.

This instrument is to be construed and interpreted as a general durable power of attorney effective immediately.

(Optional) Special Instructions: _____
_____
_____
_____

This power of attorney will continue to be effective even though I become disabled, incapacitated, or incompetent.

I agree any third party who receives a copy of this document may act under it. Revocation of power of attorney is not effective as to a third party until the third party learns of the revocation. I agree to indemnify the third party for any claims that arise against the third party because of reliance on this power of attorney.

Signed this _____ day of _____, 20____.

_____
Signature

STATE OF MAINE   )
COUNTY OF _____) ss.

Subscribed, sworn to and acknowledged before me by _____,
this _____ day of _____, 20____.

(Signed) _____
Notary

CHAPTER 16
FORM 10: POWER OF ATTORNEY OVER MINOR CHILDREN

FORM LETS PARENT GIVE POWER TO SOMEONE OVER MINOR CHILD

This form lets parent give power over minor child under 18 to someone. The form can be modified by people to let legal guardians who are not parents give power, or to cover an adult without legal capacity.

FORM GIVES POWER OVER CHILD TO ATTORNEY-IN-FACT

This form lets a parent give power over children under the age of 18 to a person called in the form the "attorney-in-fact" to let them make decisions about issues including health care, school, records, housing, discipline, food, sports, and travel. <u>Health care in case an emergency happens is probably the main reason to do this form.</u> This can let a friend, relative, teacher, or some other person help watch a child. The form can help in many situations when a parent and child are apart, like for school, travel, family visit, work, prison, rehab, sports, or medical care (like if a parent can't always be at a hospital a child is staying in). The parent doing the form <u>keeps power and can over-rule any decision and cancel the form</u>. By law the form is <u>only valid for 12 months from date of signing</u> and then must be done again. The form gives no power over marriage, custody, or adoption or a child's money and property. The form is not usually used for short periods like a few day stay with relatives or a night with a babysitter.

It may help understanding to see the main law authorizing this form, which in it's main part says:

18-C Maine Revised Statutes § 5-127. Delegation by parent or guardian

1. Delegation; power of attorney. A parent or a guardian of a minor or individual subject to guardianship, by a power of attorney, may delegate to another person, for a period not exceeding 12 months, any power regarding care, custody or property of the minor or individual subject to guardianship, except the power to consent to marriage, adoption or termination of parental rights to the minor.

A delegation of powers by a court-appointed guardian becomes effective only when the power of attorney is filed with the court.

A delegation of powers under this section does not deprive the parent or guardian of any parental or legal authority regarding the care and custody of the minor or individual subject to guardianship.

A delegation of powers under this section is subject to the same court supervision that applies to temporary substitute guardians as described in section 5-124, subsection 5.

Any delegation under this section may be revoked or amended by the appointing parent or guardian in writing and delivered to the person to whom the powers were delegated and to other interested persons.

PEOPLE MUST SIGN FORM BEFORE NOTARY

For the form to be valid it should be signed by 1 parent before a notary who then notarizes the form. Some people modify the form so 2 parents can sign so it seems more impressive and likely to be followed. The form can be kept till needed or hand it out to the person given power in the form. In the rare event someone wants to cancel the form (instead of just waiting for it to end) people should tell everyone it is cancelled and then send a page with a sentence saying the form is revoked to the person given power.

POWER OF ATTORNEY OVER MINOR CHILDREN

KNOW ALL PERSONS that I, _____, of _____, Maine, appoint _____, of _____, Maine, to be my lawful attorney-in-fact regarding my minor child[ren]:

_____ born on _____
_____ born on _____
_____ born on _____.

I hereby grant to my attorney-in-fact named above **all of my powers regarding the above-named children** including care and custody, except my power to consent to marriage or adoption and except my power to sell, transfer, convey or otherwise manage any real or personal property belonging to or involving my minor child[ren].

I hereby intend that my attorney-in-fact have the same full authority as I have to consent to, or withhold consent to, any medical or other professional care, counsel, treatment or service to said minor child[ren] by a licensed or certified professional person or institution engaged in the practice of, or providing, a healing art. I also hereby intend my attorney-in-fact have the same authority as I have to consent to, enroll, and request schooling at any place or facility for said minor child[ren].

The rights, power, and authority herein granted shall remain in full force for 12 months from date this documents appears signed below or until terminated by a written Revocation of Power of Attorney signed by me, whichever happens first.

This Power of Attorney shall not be affected by my disability or incapacity. The authority herein granted to my attorney-in-fact named above is exercisable by him or her, notwithstanding my later disability or incapacity or later uncertainty as to whether I am dead or alive. A copy of this document is as good as the original and may be relied upon.

IN WITNESS WHEREOF I have hereunto set my signature this _____ day of _____, 20____,

Signed:_____

STATE OF MAINE
COUNTY OF _____, ss.

Personally appeared the above named _____ and acknowledged the foregoing instrument to be his free act and deed.

Before me,   _____
                                         Notary Public

CHAPTER 17
FORM 11: GRANT OF CUSTODY AND CONTROL OF REMAINS AFTER DEATH

LETS PERSON BE NAMED TO CONTROL FUNERAL AND RELATED MATTERS

This form lets a person be named to later control disposition of a dead body, funeral, burial, cremation, and related matters. This form is rarely done. This book's form is based on forms funeral homes use.

IN FORM CAN NAME FUNERAL REPRESENTATIVE TO SAY WHAT TO DO

In the form a person can be named "Authorized Person" to later control the funeral, burial, cremation, and related details. If this form isn't done then by law closest family control things starting with decedent's spouse, adult children, parents, and then siblings. But most people skip this form and only do this form if it is likely that family may do unwanted things, be too upset while mourning, or be bad with money. The form has a space to write instructions but many people skip this and trust the family and others to do what the person said was wanted. Some people write to stress they want low cost, and some write to ask for "Direct Burial" or "Direct Cremation" which is cheap but is done fast without ceremony and family watching. Basically, all people usually should do what the decedent who died wrote or clearly said they wanted if the money and property in decedent's estate can afford it. Payment for things comes from pre-paid funeral accounts, insurance, and decedent's or estate's money and property, and the Executor and family by law must help arrange payment.

TO COMPLETE FORM IT JUST MUST BE SIGNED AND DATED

The form to be complete just must be signed and dated, and no witnesses or notary are needed at all. The form should be kept so it will be found very quickly after death (usually within 1 or 2 days) or it can be given immediately to someone to hold.

GRANT OF CUSTODY AND CONTROL OF REMAINS AFTER DEATH

I, _____ (name), born _____ (date of birth) being of sound mind, give custody and control of my bodily remains after my death, including the right to make all decisions regarding the handling of the dead body of mine, possession, at-need funeral arrangements, cremation, funeral, ceremonies, and final disposition and disinterment, to the following individual who shall be called the "authorized person":

Name _____ Phone _____

Address _____

I hereby give the following instructions:

_____

_____

_____

_____

_____

_____

_____

_____

_____

SIGNATURE

This document is authorized by state law, including 22 Maine Revised Statutes §2843-A. I sign this document voluntarily and I understand its purpose.

_____ _____ _____
Signature   Date   Phone

Address: _____

APPENDIX:
HOW TO GET FORMS AND SAMPLE FILLED OUT FORMS

TO GET FORMS TO USE PEOPLE CAN:
- (1) PHOTOCOPY BOOK PAGES,
- (2) TEAR OUT PAGES FROM A BOOK, OR
- (3) DOWNLOAD BOOK WITH FORMS FROM WWW.DAVENPORTPUBLISHING.COM

AND **USUALLY A PDF FORM AT IS BEST** TO AVOID SPACING/FORMAT CHANGES.

EMAIL ANY COMMENTS TO DAVENPORTPRESS@GMAIL.COM.

On the next pages to show how it can be done are some filled out legal forms which are shown as samples so people can see how it is done.

People can add words to legal forms by computer or typewriter to be neater, but many people just by hand use pen, marker, or pencil to handwrite words into forms.

It is not required but is bit better if signatures are in ink or marker not pencil.

Many parts of the forms especially Will gifts can be left empty and unfilled.

Anyone can fill in words in legal form not just the person doing the form, like a friend who has neat writing can fill in all the words, addresses, and dates that are needed. **Only the final signatures must be done by each person who is doing the form**.

To add words in form by pen, pencil, typewriter, or computer any of these is fine:
"I appoint ___*John Doe*___ as Agent",
"I appoint ___John Doe___ as Agent",
"I appoint John Doe as Agent".

When doing forms it may help to know "respectively" means "in order just stated".

People need not worry about neatness or small mistakes, and a document is usually fine if those people who knew a decedent in life can tell the likely meaning.

**Sample Filled Out Form: Last Will and Testament (Standard)
with Gifts section skipped to not bother making small gifts**

LAST WILL AND TESTAMENT

I, _Paul Samuel Maxwell_, of _Aroostock County_, Maine, do revoke all prior Wills and testamentary documents and do make, publish, and declare this as my Will. I am of sound mind and under no duress or undue influence and acting voluntarily.

1. LIST OF SPOUSE AND CHILDREN. To help show I am mentally competent and have sufficient memory to make a Will I wish to list any living spouse and living children I now have. I currently have the following living spouse and living children:

none

2. GIFTS. I give these gifts in this Will, but to get a gift in this section the recipient must survive me except as otherwise stated below.

I give _____ to _____.
I give _____ to _____.
I give _____ to _____.
I give _____ to _____.
I give _____ to _____.
I give _____ to _____.
I give _____ to _____.

3. SEPARATE WRITINGS. I may do writings separate from this Will to gift tangible personal property as allowed by state law, and all such writings should be followed. But any such writing not found within 90 days of my death is canceled and has no effect. A gift in such a writing to a person who does not survive me is canceled and has no effect. This Will does not revoke any such writings that now exist.

4. RESIDUE. I give the rest and residue and remainder of my estate, my money and property of any kind and nature, and anything I have an interest in so long as it was not transferred by other Will provisions (all of which is called the "residue"), as follows:

a) to _Susan Lee Maxwell my sister_ who survive me with persons just named who survive me taking the share of non-survivors, then if anything remains

b) to _Oscar David Maxwell and Jennifer Judy Tabor_ and if any of those just named do not survive me their part goes to their lineal descendants, per stirpes.

5. ADMINISTRATION. I nominate and appoint _Susan Lee Maxwell_ as Personal Representative including for me, my Will, and my estate.

6. MISCELLANEOUS. The following applies to this Will and generally.

In this Will no part left unfilled is a mistake including spaces in the residue clause.

The facts support and I want Maine state law to apply to this Will and my estate.

I order that my just debts, funeral and related expenses, and taxes be paid as soon after my death as practical but only those items my Personal Representative chooses to pay.

Priority of Will gifts of the same type is based on the order they are written.

The words "give" and "gift" also means a devise, bequest, grant, legacy, or similar.

I am intentionally not providing by Will or other ways for some family, including I am not providing for some children of mine and also children of a deceased child of mine.

If a gift Will reasonably mentions survival then survival is an absolute condition and anti-lapse laws or similar provisions have no effect and without survival the gift lapses. Unless a Will gift specifies otherwise if a Will gift goes to multiple recipients if any do not survive me the part to them lapses and instead goes to other surviving recipients.

No earlier transfer reduces a Will gift unless I usually called it a loan or advancement.

In this Will any gender or gendered word includes all genders, and the singular includes the plural and vice versa, and "they" can mean a single person or many persons.

Unless a Will specifically says otherwise a secured debt including a mortgage or lien shall not be paid off including by a Personal Representative or in probate, and a recipient of a Will gift of property takes it subject to debts. Also, no recipient of property who may lose it or who pays to keep it may have my estate or others pay or do exoneration.

If during my life I disposed of an item in a specific gift then the gift is extinguished.

I request and authorize any informal, summary, and quick probate or similar action. Any Personal Representative may act independently with no supervision of any court, including independent administration, and with no inventory, appraisal, or other action.

I give any Personal Representative the a) fullest authority, discretion, and powers allowed by state law, b) power to lease, sell, mortgage, convey, or keep property including real property in a manner and time they deem helpful or proper, and c) authority to settle or pay claims or debts in the time and manner they choose. Any Personal Representative or other fiduciary shall have all powers and authorities conferred by statute or common law in any jurisdiction they may act.

Any Guardian of any type, Conservator, Custodian, or other person managing a minor's property or money may use or invade the principal and sell property without court action.

If context permits the terms Personal Representative and Executor and Administrator are interchangeable, Conservator and Guardian of the Estate and Guardian of Property and Custodian are interchangeable, and residue and residuary are interchangeable. Any such person may stand in the place of and have all powers like the others named here.

The residue includes lapsed or failed gifts, insurance paid to the estate, digital assets, inheritances owed me, and all I had power of appointment or testamentary disposition over.

Any Personal Representative may access, manage, delete, modify, transfer, and otherwise control any digital accounts and assets I had any interest in or power over.

Any Personal Representative, Executor, Administrator, Guardian of any type like for a person or estate, Conservator, Custodian, and any other fiduciary under this Will or otherwise shall qualify and serve without bond, surety, security, surety bond, or similar.

If evidence does not show it likely a person survived me by 120 hours (5 days) then for this Will and my estate they shall be deemed in all ways as having died before me.

If part of this Will is by law invalid or unenforceable other provisions remain in effect.

Any Personal Representative may at any time transfer money or property of a minor under age 18 to a Custodian to serve under the Maine Uniform Transfers to Minors Act or similar law anywhere, and may pick a person to be Custodian including themselves.

TESTATOR

IN WITNESS WHEREOF, I declare and publish that this instrument is my Will which I make as Testator, that I do this as a free and voluntary act for the purposes expressed therein, that I am at least 18 years of age and of sound mind and under no constraint or undue influence, and I do sign this instrument voluntarily as my Will in the presence and sight of each of the persons acting as witnesses who are named and who sign below, this 8th day of June, 2022.

Paul Samuel Maxwell
Testator signature

WITNESSES

We, the persons signing below, declare that in the presence and sight of each of us persons that *Paul Samuel Maxwell* as Testator did voluntarily publish, declare, and sign the foregoing instrument as the Will of the Testator, that to the best of our knowledge the Testator is at least 18 years of age and of sound mind and under no constraint or undue influence, that each of us persons who sign below is at least 18 years old and fully competent to act as witnesses, and that in the presence and sight of Testator and each other we sign our names to witness this Will at the Testator's request.

Susan Ann Moon   14 2nd St., Houlton ME 04338
Signature of Witness #1   Address of Witness #1

Eve Mable Walker   35 Buffalo Road, Denver, Colorado 80101
Signature of Witness #2   Address of Witness #2

**Sample Filled Out Form: Last Will and Testament (Guardian)
with many gifts in Gifts section, Guardian Clause used, and Residue Given By Percentages**

LAST WILL AND TESTAMENT

I, __Paul Brian Baker__, of __Penobscot County__, Maine, do revoke all prior Wills and testamentary documents and do make, publish, and declare this as my Will. I am of sound mind and under no duress or undue influence and acting voluntarily.

1. LIST OF SPOUSE AND CHILDREN. To help show I am mentally competent and have sufficient memory to make a Will I wish to list any living spouse and living children I now have. I currently have the following living spouse and living children:
_____Ruth May Baker wife_____Oscar Elliot Baker young son_____
_____ Karen Lisa Lundy daughter_____ Derek Rupert Baker son _____.

2. GIFTS. I give these gifts in this Will, but to get a gift in this section the recipient must survive me except as otherwise stated below.

I give _____big oak table_____ to _____Anne J. Smith_____.

I give __$5,000 and Ford Truck__ to __Loretta Marsha Baxter__.

I give __buildings, land, and fixtures at 63 Wentworth Road, Bangor, Maine,__ to __Kenneth Alan Ford__.

I give __all real property and fixtures I own in Cumberland County in Maine__ to __Amy Marie Fox and Pamela Sue Fox__.

I give __903 Iceberg Road, Anchorage, Alaska__ to __James Eric Hanson__.

I give __Irish jewelry and my wedding ring__ to __Mary Natalie Swanson__.

I give __all jewelry not given above__ to __Kay Baxter and Mary Baxter__.

I give __$781.35__ to __Mary Natalie Swanson and Kevin Kilby__.

I give __Wells Fargo acct ending in #8923__ to __Lawrence Deer a hunting buddy__.

I give __all spare tires and auto parts__ to __Victor Perez my mechanic__.

3. SEPARATE WRITINGS. I may do writings separate from this Will to gift tangible personal property as allowed by state law, and all such writings should be followed. But any such writing not found within 90 days of my death is canceled and has no effect. A gift in such a writing to a person who does not survive me is canceled and has no effect. This Will does not revoke any such writings that now exist.

4. RESIDUE. I give the rest and residue and remainder of my estate, my money and property of any kind and nature, and anything I have an interest in so long as it was not transferred by other Will provisions (all of which is called the "residue"), as follows:

a) to _____Ruth May Baker_____ who survive me with persons just named who survive me taking the share of non-survivors, then if anything remains

b) to __45% to Oscar Elliot Baker, and 45% to Karen Lisa Lundy, and 10% to Hector Sanchez my friend from the Army_____ and if any of those just named do not survive me their part goes to their lineal descendants, per stirpes.

5. ADMINISTRATION. I nominate and appoint __Ruth May Baker_____ as Personal Representative including for me, my Will, and my estate.

6. GUARDIAN. I name, nominate, and appoint _Amanda Sue Brubaker my sister_ to be Guardian of any minor child of mine and to have care, authority, custody, and other control of them. I also name this same person to be Conservator for any minor child and to have care, control, and power over their property, money, and estate.

7. MISCELLANEOUS. The following applies to this Will and generally.

In this Will no part left unfilled is a mistake including spaces in the residue clause.

The facts support and I want Maine state law to apply to this Will and my estate.

I order that my just debts, funeral and related expenses, and taxes be paid as soon after my death as practical but only those items my Personal Representative chooses to pay.

Priority of Will gifts of the same type is based on the order they are written.

The words "give" and "gift" also means a devise, bequest, grant, legacy, or similar.

I am intentionally not providing by Will or other ways for some family, including I am not providing for some children of mine and also children of a deceased child of mine.

If a gift Will reasonably mentions survival then survival is an absolute condition and anti-lapse laws or similar provisions have no effect and without survival the gift lapses. Unless a Will gift specifies otherwise if a Will gift goes to multiple recipients if any do not survive me the part to them lapses and instead goes to other surviving recipients.

No earlier transfer reduces a Will gift unless I usually called it a loan or advancement.

In this Will any gender or gendered word includes all genders, and the singular includes the plural and vice versa, and "they" can mean a single person or many persons.

Unless a Will specifically says otherwise a secured debt including a mortgage or lien shall not be paid off including by a Personal Representative or in probate, and a recipient of a Will gift of property takes it subject to debts. Also, no recipient of property who may lose it or who pays to keep it may have my estate or others pay or do exoneration.

If during my life I disposed of an item in a specific gift then the gift is extinguished.

I request and authorize any informal, summary, and quick probate or similar action. Any Personal Representative may act independently with no supervision of any court,

including independent administration, and with no inventory, appraisal, or other action.

I give any Personal Representative the a) fullest authority, discretion, and powers allowed by state law, b) power to lease, sell, mortgage, convey, or keep property including real property in a manner and time they deem helpful or proper, and c) authority to settle or pay claims or debts in the time and manner they choose. Any Personal Representative or other fiduciary shall have all powers and authorities conferred by statute or common law in any jurisdiction they may act.

If part of this Will is by law invalid or unenforceable other provisions remain in effect.

Any Personal Representative may at any time transfer money or property of a minor under age 18 to a Custodian to serve under the Maine Uniform Transfers to Minors Act or similar law anywhere, and may pick a person to be Custodian including themselves.

TESTATOR

IN WITNESS WHEREOF, I declare and publish that this instrument is my Will which I make as Testator, that I do this as a free and voluntary act for the purposes expressed therein, that I am at least 18 years of age and of sound mind and under no constraint or undue influence, and I do sign this instrument voluntarily as my Will in the presence and sight of each of the persons acting as witnesses who are named and who sign below, this _30th_ day of _December_, 20_21_.

Paul Brian Baker
Testator signature

WITNESSES

We, the persons signing below, declare that in the presence and sight of each of us persons that ___Paul Brian Baker___ as Testator did voluntarily publish, declare, and sign the foregoing instrument as the Will of the Testator, that to the best of our knowledge the Testator is at least 18 years of age and of sound mind and under no constraint or undue influence, that each of us persons who sign below is at least 18 years old and fully competent to act as witnesses, and that in the presence and sight of Testator and each other we sign our names to witness this Will at the Testator's request.

Olivia Anna Paulson   _82 Forest Road, Augusta, ME 04008_
Signature of Witness #1   Address of Witness #1

Matthew John Paulson   _82 Forest Road, Augusta, ME 04008_
Signature of Witness #2   Address of Witness #2

**Sample Filled Out Form: Last Will and Testament (Standard)
with Will modified to have less gifts and to have a 1 part residue clause**

LAST WILL AND TESTAMENT

I, <u>John David Smith</u>, of <u>Cumberland County</u>, Maine, do revoke all prior Wills and testamentary documents and do make, publish, and declare this as my Will. I am of sound mind and under no duress or undue influence and acting voluntarily.

1. LIST OF SPOUSE AND CHILDREN. To help show I am mentally competent and have sufficient memory to make a Will I wish to list any living spouse and living children I now have. I currently have the following living spouse and living children:
<u>my son Adam Michael Smith</u>

2. GIFTS. I give these gifts in this Will, but to get a gift in this section the recipient must survive me except as otherwise stated below.

I give <u>$200</u> to <u>each of my nieces and nephews so about $2,800 in total</u>.

I give <u>$900</u> to <u>Anchor Food Shelf in Portland, Maine</u>.

I give <u>$800</u> to <u>my old church Sacred Heart in Mesa, Colorado</u>.

3. SEPARATE WRITINGS. I may do writings separate from this Will to gift tangible personal property as allowed by state law, and all such writings should be followed. But any such writing not found within 90 days of my death is canceled and has no effect. A gift in such a writing to a person who does not survive me is canceled and has no effect. This Will does not revoke any such writings that now exist.

4. RESIDUE. The rest and residue and remainder of my estate, my property of any kind and nature, and anything I have an interest in, I give to <u>Adam Michael Smith and Judy Paula Ford</u> who survive me and to the lineal descendants per stirpes of a person just named who did not survive me.

5. ADMINISTRATION. I nominate and appoint <u>Judy Paula Ford my sister</u> as Personal Representative including for me, my Will, and my estate.

6. MISCELLANEOUS. The following applies to this Will and generally.

In this Will no part left unfilled is a mistake including spaces in the residue clause.

The facts support and I want Maine state law to apply to this Will and my estate.

I order that my just debts, funeral and related expenses, and taxes be paid as soon after my death as practical but only those items my Personal Representative chooses to pay.

Priority of Will gifts of the same type is based on the order they are written.

The words "give" and "gift" also means a devise, bequest, grant, legacy, or similar.

I am intentionally not providing by Will or other ways for some family, including I am not providing for some children of mine and also children of a deceased child of mine.

If a gift Will reasonably mentions survival then survival is an absolute condition and anti-lapse laws or similar provisions have no effect and without survival the gift lapses. Unless a Will gift specifies otherwise if a Will gift goes to multiple recipients if any do not survive me the part to them lapses and instead goes to other surviving recipients.

No earlier transfer reduces a Will gift unless I usually called it a loan or advancement.

In this Will any gender or gendered word includes all genders, and the singular includes the plural and vice versa, and "they" can mean a single person or many persons.

Unless a Will specifically says otherwise a secured debt including a mortgage or lien shall not be paid off including by a Personal Representative or in probate, and a recipient of a Will gift of property takes it subject to debts. Also, no recipient of property who may lose it or who pays to keep it may have my estate or others pay or do exoneration.

If during my life I disposed of an item in a specific gift then the gift is extinguished.

I request and authorize any informal, summary, and quick probate or similar action. Any Personal Representative may act independently with no supervision of any court, including independent administration, and with no inventory, appraisal, or other action.

I give any Personal Representative the a) fullest authority, discretion, and powers allowed by state law, b) power to lease, sell, mortgage, convey, or keep property including real property in a manner and time they deem helpful or proper, and c) authority to settle or pay claims or debts in the time and manner they choose. Any Personal Representative or other fiduciary shall have all powers and authorities conferred by statute or common law in any jurisdiction they may act.

Any Guardian of any type, Conservator, Custodian, or other person managing a minor's property or money may use or invade the principal and sell property without court action.

If context permits the terms Personal Representative and Executor and Administrator are interchangeable, Conservator and Guardian of the Estate and Guardian of Property and Custodian are interchangeable, and residue and residuary are interchangeable. Any such person may stand in the place of and have all powers like the others named here.

The residue includes lapsed or failed gifts, insurance paid to the estate, digital assets, inheritances owed me, and all I had power of appointment or testamentary disposition over.

Any Personal Representative may access, manage, delete, modify, transfer, and otherwise control any digital accounts and assets I had any interest in or power over.

Any Personal Representative, Executor, Administrator, Guardian of any type like for

a person or estate, Conservator, Custodian, and any other fiduciary under this Will or otherwise shall qualify and serve without bond, surety, security, surety bond, or similar.

If evidence does not show it likely a person survived me by 120 hours (5 days) then for this Will and my estate they shall be deemed in all ways as having died before me.

If part of this Will is by law invalid or unenforceable other provisions remain in effect.

Any Personal Representative may at any time transfer money or property of a minor under age 18 to a Custodian to serve under the Maine Uniform Transfers to Minors Act or similar law anywhere, and may pick a person to be Custodian including themselves.

TESTATOR

IN WITNESS WHEREOF, I declare and publish that this instrument is my Will which I make as Testator, that I do this as a free and voluntary act for the purposes expressed therein, that I am at least 18 years of age and of sound mind and under no constraint or undue influence, and I do sign this instrument voluntarily as my Will in the presence and sight of each of the persons acting as witnesses who are named and who sign below, this 21st day of June, 2023.

John David Smith
Testator signature

WITNESSES

We, the persons signing below, declare that in the presence and sight of each of us persons that __John David Smith__ as Testator did voluntarily publish, declare, and sign the foregoing instrument as the Will of the Testator, that to the best of our knowledge the Testator is at least 18 years of age and of sound mind and under no constraint or undue influence, that each of us persons who sign below is at least 18 years old and fully competent to act as witnesses, and that in the presence and sight of Testator and each other we sign our names to witness this Will at the Testator's request.

Mark Elliot Potter   2 Spruce St, Sherwood, ME 03932
Signature of Witness #1   Address of Witness #1

Ann Paula Blom   80 Oak Road, Goddard, ME 04008
Signature of Witness #2   Address of Witness #2

Sample Filled Out Form: Self-Proving Affidavit

SELF-PROVING AFFIDAVIT

(18-C Maine Revised Statutes § 2-503)

The State of Maine

County of __Cumberland__

We, __John David Smith__, __Mark Elliot Potter__, and __Ann Paula Blom__, the Testator and the Witnesses, respectively, whose names are signed to the attached or foregoing instrument, being first duly sworn, do hereby declare to the undersigned authority that the Testator signed and executed the instrument as their Will and that they had signed willingly, as their free and voluntary act, and that each of the Witnesses, in the presence and hearing of the Testator, signed the Will acting as a witness and that to the best of their knowledge the Testator was at that time 18 years of age or older or a legally emancipated minor, of sound mind and under no constraint or undue influence.

__John David Smith__
Testator

__Mark Elliot Potter__
Witness

__Ann Paula Blom__
Witness

Subscribed, sworn to and acknowledged before me by __John David Smith__, the Testator, and subscribed and sworn to before me by __Mark Elliot Potter__ and __Ann Paula Blom__, Witnesses, this __21st__ day of __June__, 20__23__.

(Signed) __William A. Smith__

_____
(Official capacity of officer)

Sample Filled Out Form: Tangible Personal Property List

TANGIBLE PERSONAL PROPERTY LIST

In this writing are gifts of tangible personal property to occur at my death, but this writing if not found by someone within 90 days of my death is canceled.

I may do many pages of these writings which should all be seen as one document. If there are conflicts among such writings the provisions of the more recent writing will revoke the inconsistent provisions of a prior writing.

If a person getting a gift below does not survive me such gift is void and canceled.

DESCRIPTION OF PROPERTY		NAME OF PERSONS TO GET PROPERTY
1998 Ford Truck	to	Samantha Bell
1.3 carat diamond ring + Irish rings	to	Ann Sue Reed
14 ft power boat + kayak + paddles	to	L. Wheeler
Amish style bench	to	Reba Stewart
glass table, telescope, umbrellas	to	Rebecca Stewart
Irish wood cups, oak platter, red vase	to	Mary and Cindy Lott
painting of sailboat in storm	to	Mary Lott
chainsaw with number 382937	to	Mary Lott
chainsaw with number 89930	to	Matt Smith
antique lanterns + repair kits	to	Sue Wu maid at Hart Hotel
lamp kept on porch	to	Mary Kay Poppler
sewing machines	to	Mary Kay Poppler
rocking chair bought in Oregon	to	Don Winkler boat mechanic
all fishing poles and fishing nets	to	Joe "Fish" Hoss, fishing pal
hats at cabin	to	Ken Baker
all clothing except hats at cabin	to	Melissa and Wendy Smith
	to	
	to	
	to	

DATE: 5-15-2024   SIGNED: John David Smith

Sample Filled Out Form: Maine Statutory Will last page Self-Proving Affidavit skipped

Maine Statutory Will

NOTICE TO THE PERSON WHO SIGNS THIS WILL:

1. THIS STATUTORY WILL HAS SERIOUS LEGAL EFFECTS ON YOUR FAMILY AND PROPERTY. IF THERE IS ANYTHING IN THIS WILL THAT YOU DO NOT UNDERSTAND, YOU SHOULD CONSULT A LAWYER AND ASK THE LAWYER TO EXPLAIN IT TO YOU.

2. THIS WILL DOES NOT DISPOSE OF PROPERTY THAT PASSES ON YOUR DEATH TO ANY PERSON BY OPERATION OF LAW OR BY CONTRACT. FOR EXAMPLE, THE WILL DOES NOT DISPOSE OF JOINT TENANCY ASSETS OR YOUR SPOUSE'S ELECTIVE SHARE, AND IT WILL NOT NORMALLY APPLY TO PROCEEDS OF LIFE INSURANCE ON YOUR LIFE OR YOUR RETIREMENT PLAN BENEFITS.

3. THIS WILL IS NOT DESIGNED TO REDUCE DEATH TAXES OR ANY OTHER TAXES. YOU SHOULD DISCUSS THE TAX RESULTS OF YOUR DECISIONS WITH A COMPETENT TAX ADVISOR.

4. YOU CANNOT CHANGE, DELETE, OR ADD WORDS TO THE FACE OF THIS MAINE STATUTORY WILL. YOU SHOULD MARK THROUGH ALL SECTIONS OR PARTS OF SECTIONS THAT YOU DO NOT COMPLETE. YOU MAY REVOKE THIS MAINE STATUTORY WILL AND YOU MAY AMEND IT BY CODICIL.

5. THIS WILL TREATS ADOPTED CHILDREN AS IF THEY ARE NATURAL CHILDREN.

6. IF YOU MARRY OR DIVORCE AFTER YOU SIGN THIS WILL, YOU SHOULD MAKE AND SIGN A NEW WILL.

7. IF YOU HAVE ANOTHER CHILD AFTER YOU SIGN THIS WILL, YOU SHOULD MAKE AND SIGN A NEW WILL.

8. THIS WILL IS NOT VALID UNLESS IT IS SIGNED BY AT LEAST TWO WITNESSES. YOU SHOULD CAREFULLY READ AND FOLLOW THE WITNESSING PROCEDURE DESCRIBED AT THE END OF THIS WILL.

9. YOU SHOULD KEEP THIS WILL IN YOUR SAFE-DEPOSIT BOX OR OTHER SAFE PLACE.

10. IF YOU HAVE ANY DOUBTS WHETHER OR NOT THIS WILL ADEQUATELY SETS OUT YOUR WISHES FOR THE DISPOSITION OF YOUR PROPERTY, YOU SHOULD CONSULT A LAWYER.

Maine Statutory Will of

John David Kent
_____
(Print your name)

Article 1. Declaration

This is my will and I revoke any prior wills and codicils.

Article 2. Disposition of my property

2.1 REAL PROPERTY. I give all my real property to my spouse, if living; otherwise it shall be equally divided among my children who survive me; except as specifically provided below: (specific distribution not valid without signature.)

I leave the following specific real property to the person(s) named:

(name)	(description of item)	(signature)
Adam Eric Kent	land in Caribou, ME	John David Kent
Ann Eve Poe	land and cabin in Eastport, ME	John David Kent
Adam Eric Kent	87 Smith Road, Bangor, ME	John David Kent

2.2 PERSONAL AND HOUSEHOLD ITEMS. I give all my furniture, furnishings, household items, personal automobiles and personal items to my spouse, if living; otherwise they shall be equally divided among my children who survive me; except as specifically provided below: (specific distribution not valid without signature.)

I leave the following specific items to the person(s) named:

(name)	(description of item)	(signature)
Adam Eric Kent	all fishing gear	John David Kent
Oscar Ramirez	brown couch	John David Kent
Peter Hart	Army medals	John David Kent

2.3 CASH GIFT TO CHARITABLE ORGANIZATIONS OR INSTITUTIONS: I make the following cash gift(s) to the named charitable organizations or institutions in the amount stated. If I fail to sign this provision, no gift is made. If the charitable organization or institution does not survive me or accept the gift, then no gift is made.

(name)	(amount)	(signature)

2.4 ALL OTHER ASSETS (MY "RESIDUARY ESTATE"). I adopt only one Property Disposition Clause by placing my initials in the box in front of the letter "A", "B" or "C" signifying which clause I wish to adopt. I place my signature after clause "A" or clause "B", or after each individual distribution in clause "C". If I fail to sign the appropriate distribution(s) or if I sign in more than one clause or if I fail to place my initials in the appropriate box, this paragraph 2.4 will be invalid and I realize that the remainder of my property will be distributed as if I did not make a will.

Property Disposition Clauses. (Select one.)

[☒ DK] A. I leave all my remaining property to my spouse, if living. If my spouse is not living, then in equal shares to my children and the descendents of any deceased child. *John David Kent*
(signature)

[ ] B. I leave the following stated amount to my spouse _____ and the remainder in equal shares to my children and the descendents of any deceased child. If my spouse is not living, that share shall be distributed in equal shares to my children and the descendents of any deceased child.

_____
(signature)

[ ] C. I leave the following stated amounts to the persons named:

(name)	(amount)	(signature)

2.5 UNDISTRIBUTED PROPERTY. If I have any property that, for any reason, does not pass under the other parts of this will, all of that property shall be distributed as follows: (Draw a line through any unused space.)

anything somehow left to Mary Kim Kent

John David Kent

(this paragraph only valid if signed)

Article 3. Nomination of guardian, conservator and personal representative

3.1 GUARDIAN. (if you have a child under 18 years of age, you may name at least one person to serve as guardian for the child.)

If a guardian is needed for any child of mine, then I nominate the first guardian named below to serve as guardian of that child. If the person does not serve, then the others shall serve in the order I list them. My nomination of a guardian is not valid without my signature.

FIRST GUARDIAN *Adam Eric Kent*   *John David Kent*
(signature)

SECOND GUARDIAN _____ _____
(signature)

THIRD GUARDIAN _____ _____
(signature)

3.2 CONSERVATOR. (A conservator may be named to manage the property of a minor child. You do not need to name a conservator if you wish the guardian to act as conservator. If you wish to name a conservator in addition to a guardian, complete this paragraph, 3.2. If you do not wish to name a separate conservator, do not complete this paragraph.)

I nominate the first conservator named below to serve as conservator for any minor children of mine. If the first conservator does not serve, then the others shall serve in the order I list them. My nomination of a conservator is not valid without my signature.

FIRST CONSERVATOR *Mary Kim Kent*   *John David Kent*
(signature)

SECOND CONSERVATOR _____ _____
(signature)

THIRD CONSERVATOR _____ _____
(signature)

3.3 PERSONAL REPRESENTATIVE. (Name at least one.) I nominate the person or institution named as first personal representative below to administer the provisions of this will. If that person or institution does not serve, then I nominate the others to serve in the order I list them. My nomination of a personal representative is not valid without my signature.

FIRST PERSONAL REPRESENTATIVE _Mary Kim Kent_ _John David Kent_
(signature)

SECOND PERSONAL REPRESENTATIVE _____ _____
(signature)

THIRD PERSONAL REPRESENTATIVE _____ _____
(signature)

I sign my name to this Maine Statutory Will on _May 2, 2022_ at _Portland_
(date) (city)
in the State of _Maine_.

John David Kent
Your Signature

STATEMENT OF WITNESSES (You must have two witnesses.)

Each of us declares that the person who signed above willingly signed this Maine Statutory Will in our presence or willingly directed another to sign it for him or her or that he or she acknowledged that the signature on this Maine Statutory Will is his or hers or that he or she acknowledged that this Maine Statutory Will is his or her will and we sign below as witnesses to that signing.

Signature _Paula Ann Bearclaw_
Printed name _Paula Ann Bearclaw_
Address _102 2nd Av., Bangor, ME 04482_

Signature _Veronia Nancy Kent_
Printed name _Veronica Nancy Kent_
Address _802 Bronx Road, New York, NY 01762_

Notary or other authorized person (optional)

Completing the following section and having all signatures acknowledged by a notary pubic or other individual authorized to take acknowledgments is optional but if completed will simplify the submission of your will to the probate court after your death.

I,_____ , the testator, on this _____ day of _____ 20___, being first duly sworn, do hereby declare to the undersigned authority that I sign and execute this instrument as my last will and that I sign it willingly (or willingly direct another to sign for me) as my free and voluntary act and that I am 18 years of age or older or am a legally emancipated minor, of sound mind and under no constraint or undue influence.

_____
Testator

We, _____ and _____ the witnesses, being first duly sworn, do hereby declare to the undersigned authority that the testator has signed and executed this instrument as (his)(her) last will and that (he)(she) signed it willingly (or willingly directed another to sign for (him)(her)), and that each of us, in the presence and hearing of the testator, signs this will as witness to the testator's signing, and that to the best of our knowledge the testator is 18 years of age or older or is a legally emancipated minor, of sound mind and under no constraint or undue influence.

_____
Witness

_____
Witness

The State of _____

County of _____

Subscribed, sworn to and acknowledged before me by _____, the testator, and subscribed and sworn to before me by _____ and _____, witnesses, this _____ Day of _____, 20___.

(Signed)_____
(Official capacity of officer)

SKIPPED

www.ingramcontent.com/pod-product-compliance
Lightning Source LLC
Chambersburg PA
CBHW060415220526
45465CB00008B/2893